I SWEAR I SAW THIS

I SWEAR I SAW THIS

DRAWINGS IN FIELDWORK NOTEBOOKS,
NAMELY MY OWN

Michael Taussig

THE UNIVERSITY OF CHICAGO PRESS
Chicago and London

MICHAEL TAUSSIG is the Class of 1933 Professor of
Anthropology at Columbia University. He is the author
of ten books, including *What Color Is the Sacred?*, *Walter
Benjamin's Grave*, and *My Cocaine Museum*, all published by
the University of Chicago Press.

The University of Chicago Press, Chicago 60637
The University of Chicago Press, Ltd., London
© 2011 by The University of Chicago
All rights reserved. Published 2011.
Printed in the United States of America

20 19 18 17 16 15 14 13   2 3 4 5

ISBN-13: 978-0-226-78982-8 (cloth)
ISBN-13: 978-0-226-78983-5 (paper)
ISBN-10: 0-226-78982-9 (cloth)
ISBN-10: 0-226-78983-7 (paper)

Library of Congress Cataloging-in-Publication Data

Taussig, Michael T.
 I swear I saw this : drawings in fieldwork notebooks, namely
my own / Michael Taussig.
     p. cm.
 Includes bibliographical references and index.
 ISBN-13: 978-0-226-78982-8 (hardcover : alk. paper)
 ISBN-13: 978-0-226-78983-5 (pbk. : alk. paper)
 ISBN-10: 0-226-78982-9 (hardcover : alk. paper)
 ISBN-10: 0-226-78983-7 (pbk. : alk. paper) 1. Anthropology—
Fieldwork. 2. Anthropological illustration. 3. Anthropology—
Methodology. I. Title.
 GN34.3 .F53T398 2011
 301.072'3—dc23

                                            2011025411

⊗ This paper meets the requirements of ANSI/NISO
z39.48-1992 (Permanence of Paper).

For Ayesha Adamo

Put all the images in language in a place of safety
and make use of them, for they are in the desert,
and it's in the desert we must go and look for them

GENET, *PRISONER OF LOVE*

CONTENTS

ILLUSTRATIONS

This book is about drawings in anthropological fieldwork notebooks that I kept during my travels in Colombia over the past forty years. Well, that's how it started. But now that it's finished, I see that it's really about notebooks and one drawing.

As regards notebooks, ever since the killers came riding into town in 2001 and I published an account of that in diary form, I have been thinking about fieldwork notebooks as a type of modernist literature that crosses over into the science of social investigation and serves as a means of witness—as in *I Swear I Saw This*. They say science has two phases: the imaginative logic of discovery, followed by the harsh discipline of proof. Yet proof is elusive when it comes to human affairs; a social nexus is not a laboratory, laws of cause and effect are trivial when it comes to the soul, and the meaning of events and actions is to be found elsewhere, as in the mix of emotion and reasoning that took the anthropologist on her or his travels in the first place. Thus I felt it was time to think a lot more about the first phase of inquiry—that of the imaginative logic of discovery—which, in the case of anthropologists and many writers and other creative types, such as architects, painters, and filmmakers, to name the obvious, lies in notebooks that mix raw material of observation with reverie and, in my own case at least, with drawings, watercolors, and cuttings from newspapers and other media. Not all notebooks are like this or do that. But the potential is always there, and the notebook offers you this invitation so long as you are prepared to kindle the mystique pertaining to documents that blend inner and outer worlds.

This way of thinking about the notebook seems to me all the more fitting and fruitful because of the peculiarities of *the knowing* that anthropological fieldwork produces. The notebook provides an apt vehicle for conserving this knowledge, not so much as an inert record, but as something quite different, something alive, which is why I have used the ongoing, present inflection of that word—*knowing*—as in a *type of knowing*.

As regards the drawing, what am I doing? I really don't know. I am no art critic or historian and certainly not much of a drawer. All I can say in my defense is that the text pretty much wrote itself as a continuous reaction to that one image. Sometimes I tell people it's like lifting off the layers of an onion, one after the other—a familiar image, after all. But it is more accurate to say I was drawn along.

At this point I cannot resist clues laid down in the English language. To draw is to apply pen to paper. But to draw is also to pull on some thread, pulling it out of its knotted tangle or skein, and we also speak of drawing water from a well. There is another meaning too, as when we say "I was drawn to him," or "I was drawn to her," or "He was drawn to the scene of the crime," like Raskolnikov in *Crime and Punishment*. Drawing is thus a depicting, a hauling, an unraveling, and being impelled toward something or somebody. I will be doing this twice over, first in my drawing and then, in what I have to say about it, drawing on my drawing.

1

This is a drawing in my notebook of some people I saw lying down at the entrance to a freeway tunnel in Medellin in July 2006. There were even people lying in the pitchblack tunnel. It was 1:30 in the afternoon.

The sides of the freeway before you enter the tunnel are high there, like a canyon, and there is not much room between the cars and the clifflike walls. "Why do they choose this place?" I asked the driver. "Because it's warm in the tunnel," he replied. Medellin is the city of eternal spring, famous for its annual flower festival and entrepreneurial energy.

I saw a man and woman. At least I think she was a woman and he was a man. And she was sewing the man into a white nylon bag, the sort of bag peasants use to hold potatoes or corn, tied over the back of a burro making its way doggedly to market. Craning my neck, I saw all this in the three seconds or less it took my taxi to speed past. I made a note in my notebook. Underneath in red pencil I later wrote:

I SWEAR I SAW THIS

And after that I made the drawing, as if I still couldn't believe what I had seen. When I now turn the pages of the notebook, this picture jumps out.

If I ask what grabs me and why this picture jumps out, my thoughts swarm around a question: What is the difference between seeing and believing? I can write *I Swear I Saw This* as many times as I like, in red, green, yellow, and blue, but it won't be enough. The drawing is

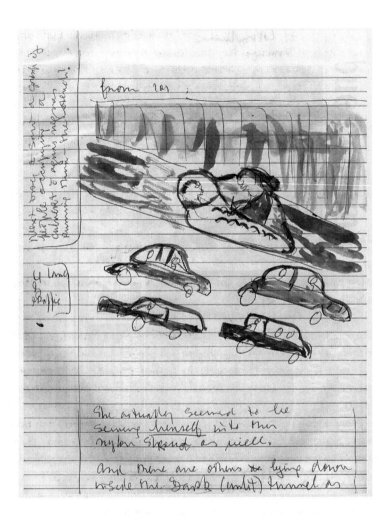

more than the result of seeing. It is a seeing that doubts itself, and, beyond that, doubts the world of man. Born of doubt in the act of perception, this little picture is like a startle response aimed at simplifying and repeating that act to such a degree that it starts to feel like a talisman. This must be where witnessing separates itself from seeing, where witnessing becomes holy writ: mysterious, complicated, powerful. And necessary.

Looking at this drawing, which now surpasses the experience that gave rise to it, my eye dwells on the mix of calm and desperation in making a shelter out of a nylon bag by the edge of a stream of auto-mobiles. I am carried away by the idea of making a home in the eye of the hurricane, a home in a nation in which it is estimated that close to four million people or one person in ten are now homeless due to paramilitaries often assisted by the Colombian army driving peasants off the land. If you consider just the rural population, which is from where most of the displaced people come, the figure is more like one in four, such that by October 2009, an estimated one hundred and forty thousand people had been murdered by paramilitaries.[1]

I might add that of all the large cities in Colombia, Medellin is, to my mind, the most associated with paramilitaries. There is a magnetic attraction between the two, and it is not by chance that in this city in particular I would witness the attempt to make a home in this freaky no-man's-land on the side of the freeway.

Three years after I saw these people by the freeway tunnel, the BBC reported in May of 2009 that soldiers in the Colombian army were murdering civilians and then changing the clothes of the corpses to those of guerrilla fighters so as to boost their guerrilla "kill count."[2] Newly applied free-market policies in the army reward individual soldiers with promotions and vacations according to the number of "terrorists" they kill. They get new language as well, the corpses be-ing referred to by the army and its critics as *false positives*. The cur-rent president, Juan Manuel Santos, was the person overseeing this program in his capacity as minister of defense. He was elected by a landslide in June 2010.

The BBC report claims that 1,500 young men have been killed this way, with more cases being notified daily. Most of them occur in the province of Antioquia, the capital of which is Medellin. "It is alleged that soldiers were sent to the city of Medellin to round up homeless people from the streets who were later presented by the army as reb-els killed in combat."[3]

They have no land but no-man's-land.

Once there was forest. They cleared the forest and grew plantains and corn. Then came the cattle. Everyone loves cattle. There is some-thing magical about cattle. From the poorest peasant to the president of the republic, they all want cattle and they always want more—more cattle, that is. The word "cattle" is the root of *capital*, as in *capitalism*. The *communist* guerrillas saw their chance. They started to tax the cattlemen, and in retaliation the cattlemen hired killers called para-militaries to clear the land of people so as to protect their cattle and then their cocaine-trafficking cousins and friends and now their plan-tations of African palm for biofuel as well. Before long they owned a good deal more than that. They owned the mayors. They owned the governors of the different provinces, they owned most of Congress and most of the president's cabinet. The just-retired president of the republic comes from Medellin, and he too is a noted cattleman, re-tiring to his ranch whenever possible, to brand cows. Imagine a cow without a brand, without an owner! Running free in no-man's-land!

Once there was forest. Now there is a nylon bag.

The one hundred and forty thousand poor country people assas-sinated by paramilitaries, recruited and paid for by rich landowners and businessmen, must have known they were dying in a good cause, if the virulent antiterrorist rhetoric of the president of the republic from 2002 to 2010 is anything to go by. That was President Alvaro Uribe Vélez, recipient of a Simón Bolívar Scholarship from the Brit-ish Council and a nomination to become a senior associate member at the St. Antony's College, Oxford, doubtless for his scholarly acumen. As governor of Antioquia before he became president for an uncon-stitutional two terms, he fomented *Convivir*, one of the first paramili-tary groups in Colombia and certainly one of its largest. Close to the entire populations of villages have been massacred by paramilitaries these past twenty years while the army looked the other way or else supplied the names and photographs of the people to be tortured and killed and have their bodies displayed in parts hung from barbed-wire fences. The people of Naya were taken out by machete. The priest of Trujillo was cut into pieces with a power saw. The stories are le-gion. President Uribe was given the Medal of Freedom by another president, George W Bush. Otherwise it's a nice enough place, like anywhere else with people adapted to an awful situation like the pro-verbial three monkeys. I ask a poet from Equatorial Guinea who has been in Colombia twenty years what's it like back there in that dread-ful African country with its thirty plus years of dictatorship. What happens to the mindset of the people? A naïve question, no doubt. "Look around yourself right here in Colombia!" he replies. For any moment you too could answer the phone and receive an *amenaza*—a death threat—because of your big mouth, your involvement in what is identified as proguerrilla activity, your raising issues of human rights or giving a student a low grade. And why are you complaining?

Somewhere, somehow, real reality breaks through the scrim. It is speaking to you at the other end of the telephone.

There are other moments like that, small and intimate and hardly worth mentioning or measuring. They hold you transfixed. Think of the people lying by the freeway tunnel in Medellin as the taxi hurtles past, a transit both ephemeral and eternal.

What I see also is an unholy alliance or at least symmetry between the enclosed space of the automobiles rushing into the tunnel and the nylon cocoon into which the woman seems to be sewing the man. The automobile offers the fantasy of a safe space in a cruel and unpredictable world, a space of intimacy and daydreaming. Yet the automobile is also a hazard, a leading cause of death and disability in the third world. As against this, consider a home on the freeway made of nylon bags, a home that takes the organic form of the insect world, like the cocoon of a grub destined to become a butterfly.

In this vein I also discern a fearful symmetry between the nylon cocoon and the steep concrete walls adjoining the unlit tunnel of the freeway. When I ask the taxi driver why people would choose to lie there, and he responds, "Because it's warm," my question assumes the sheer unfathomability, the impossibility of imagining that human beings would choose such a place to lie down in the same way as you or I lie down in our bedrooms. My question already has built into it my fear and my astonishment that people would choose such radical enclosure. Why would you put yourself into this concrete grave? And his response, "Because it's warm," suggests that it has been chosen because of its embrace.

As I dwell on these thoughts I suspect that this hideous location is chosen because it is hideous and, what's more, dangerous. There, at least you are probably safer from attack by police, death-squad vigilantes, and other poor people.

Then there is that other type of enclosure, the one that grabs me most, that part of the picture in which the woman seems to be enclosing herself as well as the man. Stitch by stitch the outside is becoming the inside. The stitcher becomes the stitched. I am reminded of that little boy years ago in a funeral service in Bogotá who said, "I want to live in a closet." His parents were research sociologists working for the Jesuits in Bogotá, gathering and publishing statistics on political violence. They were assassinated in 1997 late at night in their bedroom by paramilitaries. The boy escaped by hiding in a closet.

All of this comes to mind when I ask myself why I drew this scene and why this drawing has power over me. But I feel something is missing in what I have said or in the way I am saying it, something that undoes or at least alters meaning along the lines of what Roland Barthes rather dramatically called "the third meaning." You've heard of the third eye and the third man. Now you've got the third meaning!

Barthes was a restless thinker. No sooner had he gotten things squared away with his semiotic theory than he found exceptions to the theory because the very act of squaring things self-destructs. What is called "theory" gives you insight. But it does so at the expense of closing off things as well. Theory can never do justice to the contingent, the concrete, or the particular.[4] Yet if you don't exercise that theory muscle to the extent that you realize its limits, then you won't get to that cherished Zenlike moment of the mastery of nonmastery.

Yes! Barthes saw what he called the "information" in any given image. Yes! He saw what he called the symbolism, too. But nevertheless he became painfully aware of the shortfall between all of that and something else this act of interpretation created. "I receive (and probably even first and foremost) a third meaning," he wrote, "evident, erratic, obstinate." What's more, he spoke of being "held" by the image and that to the extent that "We cannot describe the third meaning . . . I cannot name that which pricks me."[5] Quite an admission.

Is that how a talisman works, I wonder, setting traps made of third meanings? The dangerous spirits out to get you are deflected by the design that is the talisman, kept busy trying to figure out the meaning but cannot. Their mistake. And one we repeat endlessly ourselves, too.

Third "meaning" is not really a meaning at all, but a gap or hole or hermeneutic trap *that interpretation itself causes* while refusing to give up the struggle. As such, the third meaning has an awful lot to do with the frightening yet liberating sense of enclosure as the last gasp of protection in a heartless world hell-bent on apocalypse as it roars into the tunnel of no return.

My eye fixes on the woman—if she is a woman—sewing herself into the nylon bag. And there's the stillness. Barthes recalls Baudelaire, who wrote of "the emphatic truth of gesture in the important moments of life." That is how I think of this woman's gesture, or should I say how I think of my drawing of such in which what appears as the edge of the bag as a firm blue line encloses the sewer herself. That is my gesture.

But let us for the moment remember that this is only half my story. The other half is the *act of making* the image. My picture of the people by the freeway is drawn from the flow of life. What I see is real, not a picture. Later on I draw it so it becomes an image, but something strange occurs in this transition. This is surely an old story, the travail of translation as we oscillate from one realm to the other. This is what Genet was getting at when he wrote, "Put all the images in language in a place of safety and make use of them, for they are in the desert, and it's in the desert we must go and look for them."[6] Thus Genet, the writer, enamored of images that were not really images but words. Where do such images exist then? They must exist between and within the words, on another plane, which we might as well call the desert, perhaps in the oases in the desert, as when Barthes refers us to carnival.

In an attempt to get across its skittishness, Barthes places his third meaning in the realm of puns and jokes and "useless exertions indifferent to moral or aesthetic categories," such that it sides with "the carnival aspect of things." To me, the woman sewing, apparently indifferent to the danger around her, can be equated with the realm to which Barthes points. But the carnival lies elsewhere.

For all his originality, Barthes can be seen as drawing upon an older tradition, that of surrealism, as espoused and articulated in 1929 by a German émigré living in Paris, Walter Benjamin, for whom surreal meaning has everything to do with the carnival dance of image and word. Surrealism, he said, takes advantage of the fact that life seemed worth living nowhere but on the threshold between sleeping and waking, across which, back and forth, flood multitudinous images. In this threshold situation, language opens up such that "sound and image, image and sound, interpenetrated with automatic precision and such felicity that no chink was left for the penny-in-the-slot called 'meaning.'"[7]

Like the threshold to the Medellin tunnel where the homeless lie midway between sleeping and waking, the threshold of the surrealists

between sleeping and waking is quintessentially urban, as when Benjamin writes of the "crossroads where ghostly signals flash from the traffic, and inconceivable analogies and connections between events are the order of the day. It is the region from which the lyric poetry of Surrealism reports."[8]

As for these crossroads, take another drawing I did in Medellín, where just about everyday I would witness a young man juggling sticks of fire by the crossroads under the new, elevated metro, in the hope that the passing motorists would give him money. When the lights went red—"where those ghostly signals flash from the traffic"—he would run into the middle of the four lanes of momentarily stilled traffic and begin his act. He was a terrific juggler of fire, but most of all I admired the cool way he juggled traffic, waiting to the last second before the lights changed to ask for money and leap from the path of accelerating vehicles.

Above the crossroads soars the metro. Behind courses an open sewer, a capacious concrete canal with green malodorous liquids you don't want to get close to.

Surrealism is urban. Yet what makes it surreal is Barthes's third meaning, which makes you grope for meaning when you least expect it in a taxi rushing into a tunnel in the city of eternal spring, or witnessing a young man juggling fire at the crossroads in the midst of four lanes of traffic brought to momentary rest before the next stampede.

Like a movie, I flow onward in the stream of life that pours into the tunnel. But the woman (is she a woman?) is still, her neck bent over. The man (is he a man?) is enclosed already. He is like a deep-sea diver in one of those old diving helmets with glass windows. Why is the man in the diving helmet looking at her so keenly? That man could be you.

2

So we move from contradictions and antitheses to questions. The third meaning "compels an interrogative meaning," writes Roland Barthes.

His essay concerns not drawing but film, specifically film stills, in other words a photograph ripped out of a stream of photographs making a moving picture. The still, he asserts, is the truly filmic aspect of film (well, there's a contradiction for you). And in an extensive footnote he adds that a drawing in a comic strip qualifies as well. It seems that what is crucial is the extraction of a still from a movie, whether that "movie" is a film or something drawn, such as a comic strip or animation. Yet is there not a world of difference in this regard between a photograph and a drawing?

I was struck by this when I saw a drawing in the *New York Times* of a decapitated Maori head—a real person's actual head—that the mayor of Rouen, France, wished to return to the Maori in New Zealand, but was forbidden to do so by the French government's minister of culture, who claims that the head is not a body part but a work of art.[1] The museum has been in possession of the head since 1875 and, although it has now issued a drawing of it, has prohibited photographs. The New York American Museum of Natural History has more than thirty of these heads.

Why is the drawing okay but not a photograph? For certainly the photograph of the drawing is not only okay but very awful. This is not explained in the source at my disposal—and indeed it is impossible to explain—but part of the explanation seems to be the reverence the keepers of the head in Rouen currently manifest toward it: a reverence for the dead, for the dead body, and a reflection of that shudder of

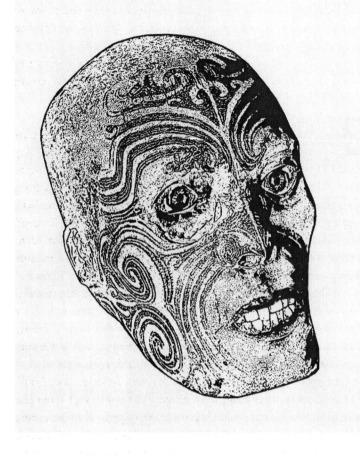

appetizing horror people can afford to turn their back on—now that we are civilized—when confronted with the macabre practice of our nineteenth-century forebears trading in the colonial exotic, which was pretty much what the Maori chiefs were doing too, selling the heavily tattooed and smoked heads of slaves to Europeans to supply a robust market. Could it be that the photograph is implicitly assumed to be a magical way of capturing the spirit of the dead, while the drawing is understood to be but a timid approximation offering no more than a squint-eyed view such that, unlike the photograph, it cannot so easily be appropriated for sympathetic magic? Something similar occurs with the use of drawings for courtroom reporting in the news media in the United States and elsewhere, the courtroom being a place where people swear to tell the truth and where photography but not drawing is prohibited.

It is impossible to say with confidence why these displacements of photography by drawing are allowed or encouraged. What's for sure is that drawing intervenes in the reckoning of reality in ways that writing and photography do not.

This struck me forcibly when I discovered what is for me a new genre—drawings in ethnographic fieldwork notebooks, namely my own and, on reflection, what little I could find of such drawings by other anthropologists and fellow travelers—Allen Ginsberg's hallucinations of The Great Being and The Vomiter in the jungles of Peru (as in William S. Burroughs and Ginsberg's *The Yage Letters*), Ginsberg's published journals, drawings by Franz Kafka in his diaries (compare with my own drawings under the spell of the hallucinogen *yagé* in the Putumayo river basin of Colombia), Walter Benjamin's drawings under the influence of hashish, Sigmund Freud's Wolf Man's drawing of his dream (although Freud ignores the drawingness of the drawing), and of course (!) my own drawings (originally in color) in such publications as *My Cocaine Museum*, *Law in a Lawless Land*, *The Magic of the State*, as well as my shamanism book, all lifted straight from my fieldwork notebooks.

These drawings surpass the realism of the fieldworker's notebook, that drive to get it all down in writing just as it was, that relentless drive that makes you feel sick as the very words you write down seem to erase the reality you are writing about. This can be miraculously checked, however, and even overturned, by a drawing—not because a drawing makes up the shortfall so as to complete reality or to supercharge realism but, to the contrary, because drawings have the capacity to head off in an altogether other direction. Whether looked at on their own or in the context of their surround of text, the drawings in notebooks that I have in mind seem to me to butt against realism, with its desire for completeness. The drawings come across as fragments that are suggestive of a world beyond, a world that does not have to be explicitly recorded and is in fact all the more "complete" because it cannot be completed. In pointing away from the real, they capture something invisible and auratic that makes the thing depicted worth depicting. And it is worth noting that these examples are of exceedingly

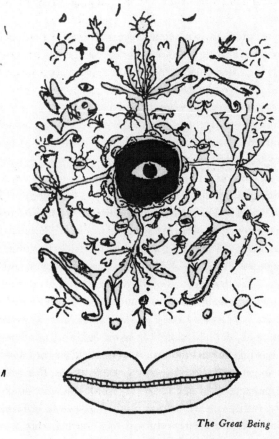

The Great Being

The Great Being

intense experiences—violence and poverty in a surreal blink of the eye in Medellin, Ginsberg's hallucinogenic experience in the Peruvian *selva*, and the Wolf Man's childhood dream charged with his fear of wolves and the scene of his parents—like wolves—having sexual intercourse when he was a tiny infant.

Of course there are anthropological fieldwork drawings and paintings (which I shall leave nameless) that painfully strive for realist representation and betray the suggestive potential that drawing possesses so abundantly. Indeed, "betrayal" hardly describes the woeful depths, even revulsion, that the studied realism I have in mind achieves. Against which, consider the following drawings that do everything a photograph doesn't. They are intimate, they are sketchy, they are suggestive, and they are metaphysical. As for my own drawings in

The Vomiter

The Vomiter

The Wolf Man's Dream

fieldwork notebooks, I have vivid memories of the copyeditor of a publishing house writing to me in connection with the drawings I wanted to include in my shamanism book, "I fail to see what these add to the text." God knows, but I persisted. Years later, an editor in the same press twisted my arm to include other drawings in other texts and even make one the cover for *Law in a Lawless Land*. And so it goes.

But to get to basics: Why draw in notebooks? In my own case, if not in others, one reason, I suspect, is the despair if not terror of writing, because the more you write in your notebook, the more you get this sinking feeling that the reality depicted recedes, that the writing is actually pushing reality off the page. Perhaps it is an illusion. But then, illusions are real too.

"The worst torment, when I try to keep a Journal," says Barthes, "is

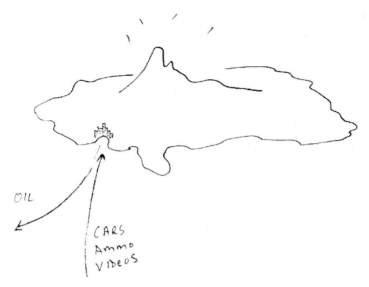

My magic of the state. A fictitious Latin American republic like Joseph Conrad's Costaguana.

the instability of my judgment. Instability? Rather its inexorably descending curve." Searching for the apt image, he cites Stéphane Mallarmé: "the flowers that fall from my mouth are changed into toads."[2]

"One Always Fails in Speaking of What One Loves" is the title of one of Barthes's last essays. It concerns the difference between what Stendhal wrote in his *journal* about Italy (a resounding failure) and the way his love for Italy came across in his *novels* (a resounding success).[3] "Any sensation," wrote Barthes, "if we want to respect its vivacity and its acuity, leads to aphasia."[4] But in Stendhal's case, at least, the novel form allows him to get around such aphasia by providing narrative, myth, beauty, and meaning—"the very transcendence of egotism."[5] Might drawings do the same?

In this regard, Freud suggested that when we perceive something, it is taken up by consciousness and, so to speak, disposed of there and then in consciousness, where it is obliterated—Yes! *obliterated!*—as is the case with the analogy he makes with a fun device popular in his day and into my childhood as well. This was the *mystic writing pad*, a celluloid sheet laid over a wax tablet such that when you write on the sheet with a stylus, the writing is clear, but once you lift up the celluloid

Cable cars, Medellin. Meeting with ex-ELN guerrillero, 2006.

sheet with your writing on it, the writing disappears—except for a faint trace on the wax tablet below.[6] In this analogy the celluloid sheet is like consciousness. It receives the imprint of the senses. All is clearly etched until consciousness "processes" the impressions and they disappear, which is what happens when you lift the celluloid sheet.

Naturally much depends on the sort of notes you are making. Ingeniously distinguishing what he calls "headnotes" and "scratch notes" from "fieldnotes," the anthropologist Simon Ottenberg believes that the headnotes—what you do *not* write down but keep inside your head—are "always more important than the fieldnotes." In his case the fieldnotes seem obsessively methodical and were typed up for careful perusal by his rather nosey professors back in Evanston, Illinois, a long way from Nigeria, where he began fieldwork in 1952. Looking back thirty years later at his three types of notes, it seems to him that the closer they were to writing, the less valuable and interesting they were. The more he actually wrote, we might conclude, the less he got. The writing machine was actually an erasing machine.[7]

What I am getting at is that the fieldwork notebook (but not the "headnotes" or the "scratch notes") is pretty much the living instantiation of Freud's mystic writing pad. Only you don't need a *mystical* pad with a celluloid cover. Any old pad will suffice, and all you have to do is write and write and watch it go down the chute. No need for that celluloid cover action. It is as if writing—the epitome of consciousness—obliterates reality, pushing it further and further out of reach. But then what I have in mind here is a special kind of writing, not poetic or literary—heavens forbid!—but the direct transmission of experience onto the page, usually hurried, abbreviated, and urgent. How tragic, then, that each word you write down changes from a flower into a toad. Each word seems to multiply the distance between you and what the word was supposed to be about.

Of course, every now and again there will be a "hit" where, with precision and vividness, words written down in feverish haste score a bull's-eye. I know this for a fact, having interpolated extracts from my diaries into my published texts for this reason, and I love their energy

My legs as viewed from my hammock (Sierra Nevada, land of the Kogis)

in their new location—like drawings, I suppose. This seems to me the very peak of perfection, where these "hit" words become images you can see in your mind's eye, see and feel, and the truth of the experience described rings whole and pure. Perhaps these "hits" belong more to Ottenberg's "scratch notes," or what Joan Didion in her essay on notebooks rather surprisingly refers to as "lies," a topic to which I shall later return.[8]

We bump into this emphatic "hit" relationship between words and images if we pause to consider not the mystic writing pad but Freud's notion of dream images as words organized into a picture-puzzle configuration. Here something like the opposite of the mystic writing pad exerts itself. Far from being erased or erasing the reality it represents, the picture-puzzle, emits power as image because it suggests secrets and, on occasion, unusual insights into the human condition. I would like you think of the drawing of the people by the freeway tunnel with this picture-puzzle concept in mind. And I would also like you to consider Benjamin's frequently expressed sentiment regarding "hit" images, which he felt flared up briefly at moments of danger in world history, only to subside if not "grasped."[9]

No matter how crude or distorted, drawing seems to impede the rush to nowhere of the mystic writing pad. This indicates a solid practical reason for drawing in a fieldwork notebook, providing psychological comfort against the sense of reality obliteration induced by writing, but then such a comfort is itself based on something whose desperation defies analysis, such as the transformation of flowers into toads. Not that I have anything against toads. The question is why or how does drawing provide comfort, if comfort be the word?

3

You might go on to ask, "Okay, if that's the case, why not use a photograph instead of a drawing or as well as a drawing? Surely you are saying that any mode of picturing or visualizing would have the same function in arresting erasure? What's so special about a drawing?" There must be many responses to this question, and ultimately none are satisfactory. But let me try, since this allows me to explore more fully what I see at stake in drawing in relation to writing.

The most obvious retort to the question of why drawings in notebooks differ from photographs is that the drawings—at least the ones I have in mind—fold organically into the writing in the notebook. You write on the page you are drawing on. It is all part of the one process, while a photograph lies in another sphere altogether with a lot of technical junk between you and the world. I like the Luddite gesture of the drawing too, the almost purposely inept make-your-own in a world of packaged perfection saturated with Photoshop-enhanced pictures.

What is more, photography is a *taking*, the drawing a *making*, and although there is much to quibble about with these words, there is wisdom in them too. John Berger certainly thinks so, with his enigmatic notion that a *photograph stops time*, while a *drawing encompasses it*—and this from a writer who has published a lot of photographs by Jean Mohr alongside text, as in Berger and Mohr's studies of guest workers in Europe and of French peasants among whom Berger lived as a guest worker (if you include writing as work, alongside his cutting and bailing hay).[1]

Encompass. Like *enclose*. But *encompass* sounds more capacious, more generous, more of a two-way movement. Like what the woman was doing to the man, sewing him into the nylon bag—*encompassing* him. But the tunnel by the freeway? That is *enclosure*. As for myself, I must be Berger's idea of the photograph, for I find myself, like it or not, trying to stop time, always returning to the scene of the crime or at least the image of the scene of the crime, by which I mean the people by the tunnel entrance.

Berger is known for his writing. Yet there is this other and less well-known Berger who seems to spend an inordinate amount of time drawing as well. To read him on drawing—to read him drawing—is to be struck by the intimacy he feels between the drawer and the drawn. His considerable love affair with photography pales by comparison, as when he suggests that drawing is like a conversation with the thing drawn, likely to involve prolonged and total immersion.

A *conversation*!

To paraphrase Berger writing on life drawing in 1960: it is a platitude that what's important in drawing is the process of looking. A line drawn is important not for what it records so much as what it leads you on to see. "Each confirmation or denial brings you closer to the object, until finally you are, as it were, inside it: the contours you have drawn no longer marking the edge of what you have seen, but the edge of what you have become . . . a drawing is an autobiographical record of one's discovery of an event, seen, remembered, or imagined."[2]

To me the crucial and alarming thing here is the idea that the person drawing becomes what they are drawing. Berger puts it so well, so subtly: "the edge of what you have become." What delight this would have caused Walter Benjamin, who begins his three-and-a-half-page essay on the mimetic faculty with these words: man's "gift of seeing resemblances is nothing other than a rudiment of the powerful compulsion in former times to become and behave like something else. Perhaps there is none of his higher functions in which his mimetic faculty does not play a decisive role."[3]

"I feel I see more than most people," declares Christopher Grubbs with regard to his drawing. "By recording the scenes before me so carefully I remember them more clearly. I become more deeply connected to the things I draw and concerned about them. A richer life issues from this more intimate relationship with the visible world . . . Drawing breathes life into an idea."[4]

For Berger, drawing is an activity much older than writing or architecture. It is as old as song, that inflection of language. Indeed "drawing is as fundamental to the energy which makes us human as singing and dancing."[5] Drawing he adds, has something that painting, sculpture, videos, and installations lack—corporeality.[6]

Others refer to this as the *kinaesthetic* sense in drawing.[7] Derrida, who does not draw, speaks of the prominence of the hands in drawings made of the blind. In many of the drawings he chooses, it is the blind person's outstretched, quavering hands that are the predominant feature. These hands are like eyes that are conversing with the immediate environment. For Derrida, this is to underline the importance of the hands not only for the blind but for the artist in the act of drawing. The parallel is disturbing, for just as the blind are pictured with their agile hands stretched out in front of their body, these hands that serve as eyes, so the artist is using her or his hands as eyes too, and with that the whole body is eye.[8]

In my drawing of the people by the freeway tunnel I see that I have pictured the woman—if she is a woman—using her hands to sew closed the nylon bag containing the man, if he is a man. Her body is bent over, her face is intently looking down at her handiwork, and there appears to be a needle in her right hand.

She is drawing herself into the picture no less than into the nylon bag.

She is drawing her entire body into this space that is the emotional and metaphysical heart of the image.

To me this is crucial. The corporeality of which Berger speaks seems to me to be like sympathetic magic in which an image of something provides the image-maker bodily access to its being. To "become and behave like something else" is the way Benjamin put it. "In order to make an image come alive, one must be totally within it," writes Chip Sullivan.[9] How marvelously dialectical this must be! You draw an image that has a mimetic relationship with what it is an image of (bear in mind this does *not* mean that there is necessarily a one-to-one resemblance, as if such a thing were possible). That is what we could call magic station number one. But coincidentally there is set up a mimetic relation between you, especially that part of you called your body, with whatever it is that is being rendered into an image, and also with the resulting image itself—magic stations number two and three!

Drawing his father's face shortly after he died, Berger felt like a lifesaver saving a life, in this case by saving a likeness. But what sort of likeness? "As I drew his mouth, his brows, his eyelids," he writes, "as their specific forms emerged from the whiteness of the paper, I felt the history and the experience which made them as they were."[10]

Because of all these possibilities—self-transformation, making an image come alive, dwelling within it, and drawing out history—it seems to me obvious that a drawing in a fieldwork notebook has a lot to offer. Even if I am looking at someone else's drawing I am likely to feel like stretching out my hand to the thing pictured. Speaking for myself, I rarely have this feeling with a photograph. Drawings are Dionysiac. Didn't Berger mention dancing?

In the West, dancing and drawing are separate activities. There are people who dance, and there are other people who draw. People of other cultures are different. In indigenous Australia, for instance, drawing on the body and on the sand both went hand in hand with dancing. Still do in some places. Hand in hand.

Yet the dancing connection seems important, even for those who never dance. To draw is to move my hand in keeping with what I am drawing, and as the hand moves, so does the body, which tenses and keeps changing the angle of vision along with the angle of the head looking out at the scene and then back at the page. This is an extraordinary act of bodily mimesis. As in certain forms of dance, your entire body imitates not just the shape but the rhythms and proportions of time held still as the page fills with figural or abstract form. You try out a line this way on the page, then change it to another. You observe keenly. Very keenly. Like never before. This is a new eye. Like a hawk. This is the golden road to realism. But then through ineptitude or quirks in your realist armor, something else takes over. Your soul, perhaps, or the soul of whatever it is that you are drawing?

This can take me anywhere from ten minutes to an hour or even longer. Other people take days. Someone told me recently that the human head weighs about ten pounds. That's a lot of weight to keep pushing around and rotating, looking at what you are drawing, then looking back at the page, ad nauseum. When I finish a drawing more elaborate than the sketch of the people lying by the freeway tunnel, I feel like I've just finished a long-distance race and I yearn for a cigarette or some other release. Of course it is not the actual physical effort that fatigues. It's the mental effort. But what then is "mental effort"?

What I think all of this boils down to as regards the fieldwork note-book or diary is the making of a fetish: the construction, guarding, cherishing, and the continuous elaboration in writing and drawing that is the notebook itself. This is a most excellent thing, I feel forced to point out, since fetishism has by and large received a lot of bad press, being associated with seedy men in shiny raincoats and old tennis shoes inhabiting the back rows of certain movie houses. Or else it is linked to the celebrated "false consciousness" of capitalist culture, mistaking things for the spirits of commodities. Or is it the other way around? In any case, endowing things with godlike powers seems to me a nice boost to the imagination required of us to navigate our way through today's nasty world. It is a boon, therefore, that the fieldworker's diary achieves fetish status, and does so in no uncertain manner.

Like ivy or some exotic weed, the diary shoots out tendrils and flowers. As the seasons proceed, so new growths form with different colors and shapes creating new patterns superimposed over the decay-ing leaves and flowers and of course those evil-eyed glistening toads that emerged earlier. Not to put too fine a point on it, the notebook becomes not just the guardian of experience but its continuous revi-sion as well, a peculiar and highly specialized organ of consciousness no less than an outrigger of the soul. It becomes an extension of one-self, if not more self than oneself. If a camera is a technical device that more often than not gets in the way—gets between me and people—the diary or fieldwork notebook is a technical device of a very differ-ent order and even more magical than the much-acclaimed magic of photography.

This would help explain the marvelously "irrational" responses re-ceived by the anthropologist Jean Jackson when asking other cultural anthropologists about their fieldnotes, as reported in her essay "I Am a Fieldnote." The fetishism of the fieldwork notebook as an "outrig-ger of the soul" could not be clearer, especially given the cruel twist she notes, almost in passing, when she asks how something could be so much a part of you and so alienating as well?[11] Is this the alienation one feels in being unable to get it down right, hence the resort to tricks such as drawing and the living scrawl of afterthoughts?

The seventy anthropologists she interviewed in the early 1980s provided a treasure trove of crazy and delightful characterizations of their fieldnotes, enlivened by the ease with which their professional lexicon came to their aid: *fetish, taboo, sacred, ritual, masking, mystique, mana, liminal quality of fieldnotes,* and *mythology of fieldnotes,* to name the more obvious.

It is indeed quite beautiful as well as startling to see the aplomb with which terms drawn from such so-called primitive societies can be applied to fieldnotes. Even the analyst of the analysts, Jackson herself, cannot avoid it, such as when she refers to the fieldworker's advisor back home as the generic shaman.[12] The irony may be plain, but so is the temptation. Nevertheless that is lightweight compared with the following extract from an anthropologist talking about fieldnotes: "When I think of activities I do, that's [i.e., writing fieldnotes] a lot closer to the core of my identity than most things. I'm sure the attitude towards the notes themselves has a sort of fetishistic quality—I don't go stroke them, but I spent so much time getting, guarding, protecting them . . . if the house was burning down, I'd go to the notes first."[13] Others comment, "it's strange how intimate they become and how possessive we are." Another says she will eventually destroy hers, and still another says, "fieldnotes are really holy." One person likes her notebooks covered with batik. They look so pretty. "On the outside. I *never* look on the inside."

Small wonder that the analyst of the analysts scratches *her* head in wonder, forced to ask why it is that so "many interviews do offer evidence of fieldwork mystique," even if a minority of those interviewed held to the view that their fieldnotes are a mere tool.[14]

Novel and Notebook, Ethnography as Literature: now the genres are churning. Consider Laura Bohannan's wondrous *Return to Laughter: An Anthropological Novel,* published in 1954 as a so-called fictional account of her fieldwork among the Tiv in Nigeria. The first edition, published by the American Museum of Natural History, blurbs this book as "a remarkable novel," presumably so the reader will keep it securely in the realm of literature and never mistake anthropology for fiction.[15] But then what is fiction? Or what is not fiction? might be the better question, since the first way of posing the question assumes a nice safe world of the real upon which and after which we create fictions. But that nice safe world does not exist. It is shot through with fiction, never more so than for that benighted being, the anthropological fieldworker, awash in floods of othernesses and daydreams of home, as this novel (I mean "novel") makes clear.

What is here fascinating is the role of the notebook that the author invokes with such frequency that it becomes a character in its own right—having a "role," after all—anchoring the outlandish and strange with pen and paper. But immediately two possibilities, two questions, arise. Is the notebook actually playing this role as a quasi-character as the anthropologist navigates her way through Tiv worlds? Or does the notebook assume this status afterward, when she is concocting her "fiction," in other words a device that a writer (as in writer-of-fiction) uses to get the story to come alive? Either way the notebook is magical. It is as magical as the curtain of witchcraft that remorselessly descends over this novel that is, be it noted, not just "anthropological" but focused on fieldwork.

"I scribbled in almost illegible haste in my notebook . . . my notebook was full of questions." "Where did the second goat come in? . . . He told me that now we were to start the real pith of the lesson. I turned to a fresh page of my notebook . . . I repeated and wrote."[16] The notebook is not only a principal character in her book, along with the chief and the sorcerer, but to my mind it conflates the two.

It is the Tiv themselves who take over the responsibilities of keeping a notebook. "Write that down! . . . He opened my notebook for me and had me write down the words for everything in our line of vision."[17] When she exploits the rift between the chief and Yabo (the most feared sorcerer), with whom nobody but she will associate, Yabo teaches her the black arts, provided she write them down in a new notebook that she promises to never show the chief.[18]

Deeply upset at a small boy taunting a blind man, she says, "I will get my paper," and goes into her hut "but not to get paper" so much as to hide from the world.[19] It is as if the paper becomes the mediator of the strange and, more than that, as if the paper is a sacred or semisacred repository. But there are limits to this capacity for buffering when even the notebook fails her, as with this display of cruelty whereby paper becomes but an excuse enabling retreat into the self.

Yet when the holocaust of smallpox rips through the community, her notebooks become an abject sign of a woeful alienation, indicating her inability to relate either to herself or to the people around her. "I had followed science out here, as one follows a will o' the wisp," she writes, "seeing only what beckoned from the distance, paying no heed to the earth I spurned beneath my feet, seeing naught about me."

She rubs salt in the wound. "But . . . I had served anthropology well. Notebook upon notebook, good stuff and accurate."[20]

And if the notebook is one of the principal protagonists in her anthropological novel, it is also the main character in the storytelling that brings her book to its finale when the community regroups after the devastation of the smallpox. Storyteller after storyteller takes the stage in what is a sort of "truth and reconciliation" hearing. The very same small boy who taunted the blind man interrupts with "What was his great grandfather's name? And where did he learn to perform that ceremony." The audience shrieks with laughter. Our anthropologist then realizes that his accent is hers, and he is imitating the Anthropologist as, eager and baffled in turns, the boy scribbles in the air "as though in a notebook."[21] Yet these very same people doubled over with laughter—with the "return to laughter"—had always been emphatic that during her time with them she write down "everything in our line of vision."

Scribbling in the air is a gesture that should not be lost on us, given the doubts and anxieties I have belabored concerning the "mystic writing pad" effect. And here I cannot resist pointing out that once— only once—in all of the twenty-three references to her notebooks and diary, she mentions she drew pictures.[22]

Yet this one scene of drawing—not writing—is instructive. It occurs as a hut is being built for her in the chief's compound, and amid the bustle of activity the elders are, as is their custom, collectively arbitrating a dispute. As they listen to the complaints and the evidence, their hands are busy. One is fitting a hoe handle. Another is twisting hibiscus fiber to make rope. And all of this is occurring so they "could keep their hands busy while their minds were on more important matters."

Surely that also applies to the drawings she makes during this time? It is justice that is being weighed as the conversation meanders and those busy hands ply their task freeing up the mind for weighty matters. "Boredom is the dream bird that hatches the egg of experience," writes Benjamin with regard to the art of storytelling and its necessary connection to manual tasks.[23] And at the heart of storytelling, as with these dispute hearings, lies the search for righteousness. "The storyteller is the figure in which the righteous man encounters himself."[24]

Yet only once does she record drawing. Nevertheless, it is "drawing" that proves to be the "really real," as when she says she has only to close her eyes and she will recall with the utmost vividness her time with the Tiv, as vivid as her childhood memories—"disconnected and unordered: small, particular incidents" consisting of a "pointillist picture."[25]

And is it not the case that the mystique of the notebooks—scribbling in the air—is heightened by the almost universal rule in the profession

to not teach the art of fieldwork and keep all discussion of it to glancing blows and informal comments out of the side of one's mouth—"Wear tennis shoes and stay away from native women" sort of thing?

What then of drawings? What sort of lifeline might they provide? Well, first of all they provide a welcome pause to the writing machine whereby another philosophy of representation and meditation takes over. It is nice to walk on two legs instead of one. Drawings add more directly to the thing-become-spirit character of the notebook as a whole, preening the fetish with loving strokes. I like drawing, and in a strange way that I do not understand it settles me into my surroundings even though the act of drawing can be unsettling. This is paradoxical. Is the drawing something like a dialogue with one's surroundings, I wonder, maybe an argument—in the sense of a dispute but also in the sense of a theory? You are getting to know your surroundings in this strange way and, even stranger, the surroundings are getting to know you. This adds up to an unstable set of interlocking forces, the main one of which is surprise. Did I really draw this? The drawing may familiarize you with the strangeness depicted. You are making your own passport to the terra incognita. But then you have to admit that the drawing is a strange thing too. It acquires its own reality. It is actually of another universe while pretending to be the reality in front of you. Purely as a picture—as "a work of art"—it has its charms and its lack of charm.

Imagination and documentation coexist—as with the watercolor I sketched of Julio Reyes's phantom boat coming upriver at night, which I heard about on the wharf at Santa Barbara on the Timbiquí River that races down the Andes to the Pacific coast of Colombia. No photograph could capture the phantasm, that's for sure. And when I look at my watercolor, done at night, depicting the reflections upside down in the dark river of the huts on the opposite bank, illuminated by their gasoline lamps, and I see (or, more properly, sense) the struggle to capture the color of the river at night, to somehow get the blue in the black, and the even greater struggle to picture the phantom boat, grey-black in the blackness of myth and fantasy, I fear all I am left with is an unsightly smudge with some yellow stain like a mustard spill. I then tell myself that the result is pitiful but the struggle worth it because I looked at color and I looked at the night and the river like I never had before and saw what I take so for granted with new eyes. Is there any activity that so rewards failure? These are toads that become flowers.

4

Given all this, is it fair that drawings in fieldwork notebooks are generally considered to be at best mere aids, steps toward a published text that obliterates all traces of them, like denying one's parentage out of shame? At issue here is not that a fieldwork notebook should supplant the book to which it gives birth, but rather a question: What is lost in translation?[1]

I am the first to admire the smooth perfection of a completed work and be irritated by the appellation of "work in progress." I do believe in the wholeness of the whole, no less than in the stupendous artificiality of a beginning followed by a middle followed by an end. Yet at the same time I very much like sleeping in a half-constructed house with, say, the roof in place but the rafters exposed and no walls, or at least no sheetrock with its sealed, smooth whiteness producing that choking feeling of the straitjacket. When a house is completed it is such a disappointment. No rafters. No mysterious hollowed-out shadow spaces above them. And nothing to hang the hammock onto and swing—which is why we like barns and sheds and find unforgettable that house raised twelve feet in the jungle with a palm-thatch roof and only two walls, open to the forest, complete in its incompleteness. (Maybe that's what makes a great book, being more barn than house?)

So if I seem to be celebrating crudeness and half-completed efforts without sheetrock, and if I go on to affirm this as the work of the amateur, I am mindful of the putrid negativity such an appellation carries in certain quarters of the land. But, like Roland Barthes, I want to emphasize the root meaning of *amator*, for the love of it. Imagine that!

We amateurs feel little hesitation in speaking, although we are not professional speakers, just as we run, although we are not professional athletes, make love, swim, or email, et cetera. Most of us even live life amateurishly. But drawing for the amateur? Off limits. Drawing is precious in every sense of the word, except for the Littlies.

But worse still than censoring certain persons as amateurs, drawing itself is censored as a second-rate activity, secondary to writing. True, we provide a closed-off playpen for the motley crew of artists, curators, art dealers, critics, collectors, and museums, a playpen in which drawing can become an extraordinarily treasured commodity, as you can gauge from the crowds that swell art museums today and the millions of dollars paid for a drawing or a painting, far more than for any book, that's for sure. All very strange.

Except for this exception, drawing is devalued in relation to reading and writing in Western culture. Even in art schools, so I am told, the teaching of drawing has been greatly diminished the past two decades, or even curtailed. My friend Nancy Goldring has fought to retain drawing on the syllabus. Her class in New Jersey is now scheduled to meet at 7:30 a.m. It is now fashionable, I hear, for artists to proudly claim, "Oh! I can't draw." (No wonder!)

This hostility toward drawing by hand has been exacerbated by the computer, but its roots in Western culture go way beyond that. What is more, side by side with the hegemony of the digital, there now seems to be a return to the soulfulness of pencil and paper—amounting to a celebration of the craft of drawing as retaliation against the machine. And there is a market for this as well. The very first sentence in a prominent New York curator's 2008 essay on drawing reads: "In today's contemporary art world, drawing is hot."[2] But this does not reflect the broader cultural history of drawing in relation to writing and to thinking.

We do everything to get children to read and write well. But why not draw too, past the age of five or six? "Our society privileges verbal skill," writes that great drawer and landscape designer Laurie Olin, "to the point that by the time they reach middle school, most people abandon other forms of mental imagination."[3] The manager of the children's department at a prominent bookstore in Washington DC, Dara La Porte, is quoted as saying in October 2010, "I see children pick up picture books and then the parents say, 'You can do better than this, you can do more than this.' It's a terrible pressure parents are feeling—that somehow, I shouldn't let my child have this picture book because she won't get into Harvard."[4] In his marvelous study of the importance to research chemists of drawings of molecules, the Nobel Prize–winning chemist Roald Hoffmann points out that "My ability to draw a face so that it looks like a face atrophied at age ten."[5] Yet diagrams and visual thinking are of enormous value in his field, as exemplified by the picture of the double helix and its place in the discovery of DNA.

Shortly after I copied Hoffman's confession, I drove to the supermarket close to where I live in upstate New York past a sign on the road. It read: "Summer Reading Camp." I guessed my five-year-old friend Carmen Albers would soon be dumped there so as to get on with life instead of drawing imaginary giraffes. As we waited for our food in a Chinese restaurant she started to draw some more, copying figures on a Chinese lacquered vase on the table. Given her interest in animals such as giraffes, what a shock to see that instead of the animals on the vase she was copying Chinese characters. Could there be a fluid continuum at work here, such that animals and writing, drawing and writing, belong to the same universe?

Three months later I saw workmen hauling up a sign to put on top of the entrance arch to Columbia University that read: "*New York Times*. Great Children's Read." At each end of the sign were childlike drawings of a child. The child on the right was carrying a book. The child on the left had a book open and appeared to be reading it. As I stared up at this sign, a professor of ancient history named William Harris tapped me on the shoulder with a smile. "Typical anthropologist," he said with a smile, "studying the life of the street."

I explained my interest in society's effort to get the little ones to read and how this poster—and it was a very large poster—used "childish" drawings so as to encourage the first steps toward the rift, at first demoting drawing, and then eliminating it altogether from the curriculum of progress. It seems like drawing is here considered to be a prehistoric stage in one's evolution, like the tail that eventually drops off between our legs. Primers for kids to learn to read and write use drawings every inch and monosyllable, every apple and orange of the way—only to erase all that visual representation once it has served its larger, more sacred task.

Nodding approvingly in the midst of the crowd, with his head tilted to one side, my friend told me that the ancient Greek word stem *grapho* means "to write *or* draw." My thoughts flashed back to Carmen.

We both beamed with pleasure, but surely mine was greater than his, for I had doubled the contingencies. First, I had accidentally come across yet another street-sign manifestation of the victory—the victory of letters over drawing—and, second, by the most beautiful coincidence I had bumped into a scholar right under the entrance to the university, now emblazoned with this exhortation to the little folk, and he—my scholar—had beautifully muddled everything for me. The kernel at which I grasped while making my way further along the footpath is what if the ancient Greek language was on the right track in having the one word for what is now divided by an insuperable gulf?

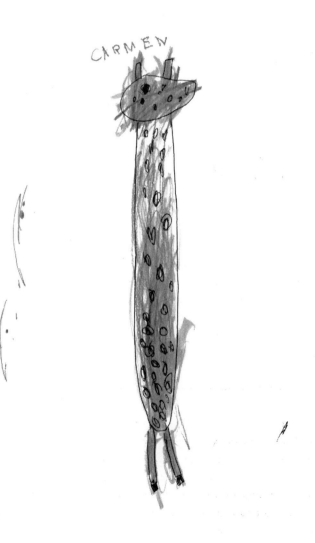

It is this same track—this same unity of writing and drawing—that we find in the Middle Ages too, when drawing was understood to be an activity that combined writing and what today we call drawing.[6] But here we have to pause because what these histories seem to reveal is that the very word "drawing" is unstable and flexible—as when I say "drawing" for my watercolors, or when I play with the multiple meanings of the English word "drawing" for making a picture, drawing water from a well, drawing a thread from a skein of wool, and of being drawn to the scene of the crime. That is the situation today. In the Middle Ages, so I read, many words connote drawing, but there is no word that signifies it *exclusively*. The relevant words refer to drawing plus something else—for example, writing. In written texts in the Middle Ages, the notion of drawing is expressed in words that convey the act of inscription, whether in letters or in pictures. One word, *scribere*, conveys the idea of making a furrow. Another, *protrahere*, from which the English *portrait* derives, suggests to disclose or reveal, which is "something a drawing can do as readily as a text."[7]

Then there are my dictionaries. While the Oxford dictionary is all words, Webster's dictionary combines words with beautiful little drawings the size of a postage stamp. In its 1,360 pages, I would guess there could be 1,360 of these drawings. My eye strays to the drawing of a horse's hoof as I read the entry under "honor." The hoof is displayed such that the parts of its underside are easily seen and named. Honor is certainly interesting, but not as interesting as this drawing of a hoof. Not only does it leap out at you but it makes you ask how on earth a purely verbal description could get even close to this, bearing in mind you can't have much honor without a hoof, but a hoof without honor is fine. What madness to rely on words! Poor Oxford. Running scared, I would say, running scared of people like me, whose eye strays to the picture away from the word, which is the same prejudice I find in my university against film as something easy and vulgar, likely to seduce students away from real learning. Yet one can only applaud the chaps who write this stuff bereft of imagery. For what an effort it must be to thus cut yourself off from the image world. But then seeing itself as guardian of the English language, and seeing that words and writing are virtually sacred, it makes perfect sense not to stoop to that vulgar American device of drawing.

Back to *grapho*!

First, I see a curious history at work here, a mythical universal history, a just-so story of my own making based on my experience as well as that of other people with whom I have discussed memories of their childhood reading. My history of reading is unabashedly Western middle class and probably pre-TV, pre-DVD, and pre-Internet—which somewhat limits my claim to a "mythical universal history." But never mind. The implications are more general, aimed at providing an archaeology in the present of the way words and pictures interact. It can be read in conjunction with Walter Benjamin's remarks on pictures in children's primers. "Prince is a word with a star tied to it," a seven-year-old boy told him.

At first the child is told stories. Then it is read to by its mother and father, usually from a lavishly illustrated children's book with but a few lines of text per page. As the child grows, so the illustrations shrink and the text spreads ever more until finally there are no more pictures. Picturing has been killed off (except the cover, which, when you come to think of it, is a very important part of a book and the object of frequent dispute between authors and their publishers). Picturing has been sacrificed in one of the most important if unannounced rites of passage on the way to being an adult. Then one fine day the kid, now aged about ten, is reading away, all is going smoothly and according to plan when, some twenty pages into a book, the kid confronts an illustration, invariably of the main character, who looks nothing—absolutely nothing!—like what the kid has in his or her imagination. Shock is followed by disorientation and depression. A mighty gap opens up between words and things, no smaller than between words and pictures. Akin to an initiation rite into epistemology, this is a decisive moment in the history of consciousness and self-consciousness that not even the mighty G. W. F. Hegel could wrap his capacious abstractions around. Something essential to the cosmic machinery of representation has fallen out of whack, after which text-and-drawings will forever be the site of a baneful disposition, scar tissue of trauma.

This scar tissue is what I see manifest in William Burroughs's and Brion Gysin's 1960s text-image collages, especially in the book they worked on together, *The Third Mind*. Sometimes Burroughs supplied the text and Gysin the images; sometimes it was the other way around. Such collages, the result of Gysin's cut-up discovery, were also sometimes built into diaries such as the *Black Scrapbook* (1964–65), a diary

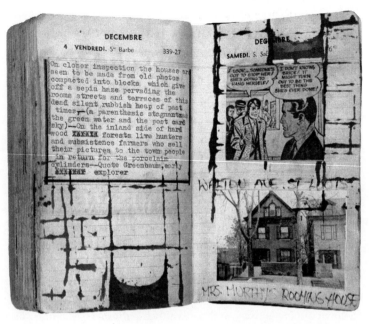

Burroughs's and Gysin's scrapbook images; pages from *The Black Scrapbook*, c. 1964–65

said to contain four hundred pages of collages.[8] Such a connection of pictures with with the diary form seems merely fortuitous, but it was sufficient to get me thinking about my own fieldwork diaries. Wasn't it possible to see them as moving in that direction, too? I asked myself, even though my notebooks were far from attaining the systematic giddiness of Gysin & Burroughs, with their obsession with outwitting Control, meaning the freaky forces of surveillance and social convention dependent upon text-image play.

Placing family photographs side by side with images cut out of American comic books of the forties and fifties, eerie images of what caught their eye, odd newspaper clippings, together with slabs of prose (if that be the word) that Burroughs was writing at the time, pithy asides, and trails of color, dividing up the page into two or three vertical columns with the day's date at the top, like a diary, Burroughs and Gysin wanted this collage to do nothing less than applied anthropology, manipulating the image world of popular culture, where language

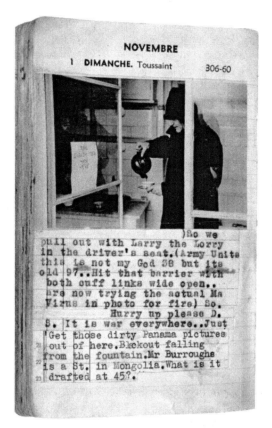

NOVEMBRE

1 **DIMANCHE.** Toussaint   306-60

)So we
pull out with Larry the Lorry
in the driver's seat.(Army Units
this is not my God 38 but its
old 97..Hit that barrier with
both cuff links wide open..
are now trying the actual Ma
Virus in photo for fire) So,
              Hurry up please D,
S. It is war everywhere..Just
'Get those dirty Panama pictures
out of here.Blackout falling
from the fountain.Mr Burroughs
is a St. in Mongolia.What is it
drafted at 45?.

Burroughs's and Gysin's scrapbook images; pages from *The Black Scrapbook*,
c. 1964–65

and image intersect. None of this occurs at a conscious level, of course.
Note the vibration effect on the page for Thursday, November 19,
Saint Elizabeth's Day.

Beyond that ambitious goal was the even larger program of erasing
the word itself. Rub Out the Word! For which reason orgasm was
recruited as well, a superior form of cut-up.[9] All this was more bom-
bast than real, in my opinion, more imaginary and tongue in cheek
than what spoilsports call "serious," recalling Burroughs's great love
of what he called "routines," little bits of theater playacted in a living room or at a bar—or on the page with iconic characters such as

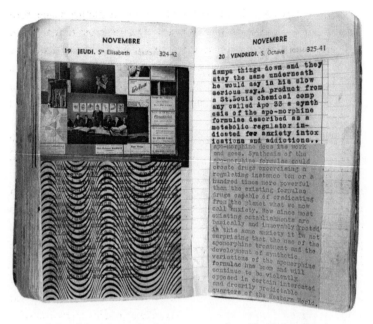

Burroughs's and Gysin's scrapbook images; pages from *The Black Scrapbook*, c. 1964–65

Dr. Benway. Recall also Gysin and Burroughs's patron saint, Hassan I Sabbah, leader of the hashish-smoking assassins (play on words): "Nothing is real; everything is permitted."

States have their routines too. Remember the weapons of mass destruction? The photographs of the mobile chemical trailers in the desert sand that the secretary of defense held up in the UN building by the East River?

The point is that in this conflation of image and language in the scrapbook, both image and word change on the anvil of conflation. Words melt into fading crosshatched grids as grammar heaves images out from the verbal realm only to sink down again under waves of effervescent possibility. In this context, the photograph of Mrs. Murphy's rooming house is like no house ever was, anymore. It is no longer a photograph, nor Mrs. Murphy's anything. The truest thing you can hang your hat on is the name of the month and the day at the top of the page—in French.

Brion Gysin, the inventor of those complementary devices—cut-up and grid—expressed it like this: "I write across the picture space from right to left and then, I turn the space and write across that again to make a multi-dimensional grid with the script I picked up from the Pan people. Who runs may read. I have, I think, paid the pipers in full. Within the bright scaffolding appears a world of Little Folk, swinging in their flowering ink jungle-gym, exercising control of matter and knowing space."[10]

Who runs may read. And also walk, as on the electric-blue mosaic tiles of the shrine in the desert dedicated to Hassan I Sabbah, Old Man of the Mountain and Great Sandy Waste. "These magic carpets in tile can catch up the soul into rapture for hours. They begin with mere optical illusion in which colors leap and swirl but the effect goes on developing to where pattern springs loose as you move into the picture you see. You step from this world into a garden and the garden is You."[11]

Who runs may read. Like Don Quixote tilting at windmills, Don William with his trusty artist friend, Brion Gysin, took on the big bad world of Henry Luce and other media moguls flooding the world with images that, as Burroughs exhorted, control us as much as do those "rings of steel" of surveillance cameras that today surround inner London, Wall Street, and your local supermarket. Whether we are being watched or whether we are watching, the end result is the same, no time more than now when media is king.

Burroughs and Gysin, writer and visual artist, made a fabulous pair, or should I say "collage," and as regards pairing up so as to create fables, it is worth recalling that Kafka would have us believe that Quixote was a bothersome spirit possessing Sancho Panza, who had to invent a bunch of adventures to keep his spirit occupied. It is said that Burroughs created some six thousand collages within three years and never stopped working eight days a week there in the Beat Hotel.[12]

Although not much of a drawer, Burroughs was encouraged by Gysin's example to take up painting, which he did in an abstract expressionist style. He never showed his work until after Gysin's death. He was slowly coming off heroin, thanks to apomorphine treatment, sitting for hours in the Beat Hotel in Paris, silently watching Gysin paint and at times seeming to disappear into the painting. After all, he was *el hombre invisible.* He was looking for the Little Folk, I am sure. "Oh, he could sit there staring into my canvases," said Gysin, "simply melting into them to move around in there."[13] Small wonder that when, twenty years later, Burroughs dedicated one of his last books, *Cities of the Red Night*, to Gysin, the dedication read: *To Brion Gysin, who painted this book before it was written.*

The voice in this book remains pretty much the same, dry and measured, but reality floats in and out of its 332 pages, hovering between pages from a notebook and pictures that come alive. "A sepia etching onscreen. Written on the bottom in gold lettering: The hanging of Captain Strobe, the Gentleman Pirate. Panama City. May 1, 1702 . . . The etching slowly comes alive, giving off a damp heat, a smell of weeds and mud flats and sewage."[14] Several chapters later a chapter begins thus: "Page from Strobe's notebook." (This same Strobe who climbed out of the painting of himself being hanged.) The text continues: "The essence of sleight of hand is distraction."[15] Well, you can say that again. Then at the bottom of that page (with us not really knowing whether we have clambered out of dead-man-come-alive Strobe's notebook), we read: "Noah writes that I am interested in printing his diaries for some reason." For some reason. Two pages on we are dropping anchor a bare hundred yards from the beach: "I had the curious impression of looking at a painting in a gold frame . . . at the bottom of the frame, April 1, 1702."[16] "The conversation at the dinner table gave me the sensation that my notebooks were coming alive."[17] "Could I see that postcard in the window?" "As I touched the picture, I got a whiff of the fever smell. Three youths were hanging from a pole."[18]

What I think Burroughs's scrapbooks added up to was one vast drawing—that half-completed house I was talking about, the one without sheetrock and with exposed crossbeams from which you can hang your hammock. His scrapbooks rehearse that moment I describe in my "mythic universal history" as that prepubertal shock occurring in the latency period between the devolving image and the evolution of reading.

He certainly was an inveterate photographer. Not only did he snap away, but in those early days, as he told the *Paris Review* contributor with the unlikely name of Conrad Knickerbocker in 1965, he kept the prints of his many photographs in heavy files that he lugged from place to place back and forth across borders and oceans to roomy rooms where he could spread out and gaze at them to his heart's content as if they were more real than reality. I have studied these files in the recently acquired collection in the New York Public Library, where they are treated like the crown jewels—a strange fate for the iconoclastic William Seward Burroughs of notoriety, literary and otherwise. Looking at the files in such surroundings, you feel like you are sitting in a bank vault or in a prison, talking to a prisoner during visiting hours. Doubtless this would have tickled Burroughs. You rifle through piles of black-and-white three-by-five photographs and travel through time and across continents. You don't just look, of course, but what is looking, anyway? You try to imagine how Burroughs looked at these photographs and you try to do the same, only now the exalted status of the outlaw writer as a cultural icon gets between you and what you are looking at and looking for. Were his photographs winking at him with concealed messages about secret events, both past and yet to come? I certainly got that feeling as I opened up the file containing spooky blurred photographs he took of TV shows in his hotel room in the Midwest. The photo collages swarm before you, page after page, creating cascading megacollages, all the more strange on account of their banality and their remoteness in time and place. Here in the prison house of the reading room you cannot but create your own scrapbook out of these raw materials in relation to the protocols of white gloves, soporific scholasticism, and frosty looks.

Yet he was first and foremost a writer, was he not? He himself had written the following: "Brion frequently remonstrated with me to leave these experiments and write some straight narrative"?[19] And as late as 1976 Gysin adds, "I would still urge him to do so."[20] Coming from Gysin, champion of experiment, this is strong stuff. Be a writer, William! Write straight, for God's sake! This seems to have only accelerated Burroughs in the opposite direction, that of time-space dislocation, as he cut out images and text for his scrapbooks. Quixote no doubt got similar advice from Sancho, but went on tilting at those windmills.

5

All of this, I repeat, seems to me curious, obscene, terrifying, and unfathomably mysterious.

JAMES AGEE ON FIELDWORK IN *LET US NOW PRAISE FAMOUS MEN*[1]

A fieldwork diary is like a scrapbook that you read and reread in different ways, finding unexpected meanings and pairings as well as blind alleys and dead ends. In thinking about it, I am reminded of how a small child plays for hours arranging and rearranging blocks and marbles, toy animals and postage stamps. Then the life in the collection crackles. Then we sense what Walter Benjamin meant when he said that a true collection amounts to a *magic encyclopedia*. What he meant was that because it is the offspring of both design and chance, a collection can function like a fortuneteller's wheel.

In part this is the product of the inordinate love and fascination—that quiet fanaticism—by which the collector gathers and regards the bits and pieces that make up his or her collection. Well do I recall the shock I received upon going into Alina Enggist's bathroom in New York City to find the washbasin virtually unusable because it was filled with small stones of different shapes and colors, the basin being one of the places she uses to house her collection of stones. To my mind this is analogous to Burroughs's scrapbooks no less than to a fieldworker's notebook.

Alina writes: "The stones of my collection do not all recall a story, a moment, or a significance. The ones that traveled far lay next to the ones that had no idea how they got there. They are all at rest, some huddled together, others alone, but all carried to where they now lay. And their Way is not yet determined as mine is not. To know that they were there before me and will be there after me is comforting. To know that their stories are not bound to them and that they may or may not ever speak again is what makes them so valuable. To know that they were carried from a moment in my life now extinct gives them their stability. Knowing that they were passed over until the moment I came and collected them gives to me a sense that I found a dream that has yet to be dreamt."

Well, an ethnographer's notebook is not quite the same as Alina's washbasin full of stones, but from her commentary you get the inside story of what lies at the heart of any collection, including what goes into a fieldworker's notebook. Of course there are fieldworkers who work with a strict plan of investigation, which is what the granting agencies insist they manifest *before* they even go into the field. The notebooks of such investigators are devices to eliminate chance as well as that magic-encyclopedia effect beloved by Benjamin, who insisted that the best way to know a city was to get lost in it. I can imagine the success this methodology would receive from the National Science Foundation and others reviewing students' grant applications.

Let us pause to consider the first thing anthropology graduate students I know are taught about grant writing, which is never to write in the first person. Invariably the application strides center stage, the applicant becoming a phantom. Invariably the application begins not with "I wish to study . . . ," but with "This project is aimed at . . ." In one stroke anything subjective is not so much erased as it is disguised and distorted by this language. The entire procedure is dishonest because fieldwork is essentially based on personal experience and on storytelling and not on the model of laboratory protocols. With the repression of subjectivity goes the repression of chance effects too. Written in the third person and passive tone, "This project is aimed at . . . ," everything is nailed down, and there will be few surprises upsetting this little apple cart. But then the laboratory thing is a charade, anyway, a ritual in which few believe—which makes it dishonest in an especially insidious way, that of a "public secret," like the emperor's new clothes.

Because fieldwork is actually based on personal experience and on storytelling and not on the model of laboratory protocols. Try to imagine the scene of the anthropologist in the field talking with someone about something. For example, myself talking with a labor contractor or a cook in the plantation fields about men who are said to make a pact with the devil to cut more cane than they can without such a pact—so the story goes. The conversation is likely to dwell on things heard and overheard, on the vagaries of people and their lives in concrete detail, and it's likely to tease the point with still another story. It is hard to imagine any such "fact" outside of its story. But what happens next is betrayal. The story is lost in its conversion to "information" or, worse still, to "data," these being the stepping stones toward the holy grail of the General and of the Abstract, that beloved X-ray way of Knowing raised on the shoulders of sensuous immediacy. Much of anthropology, certainly most that is funded, thus turns out to be telling other people's stories without realizing that's what you are doing, and telling them badly, very badly indeed—because, like drawings, such stories are seen as mere steps toward the Greater Truth of the Abstraction. This is why the fieldworker's notebook, with at least one foot in the art of sensuous immediacy, is so valuable as an alternate form of knowledge to what eventually gets into print.

And personal experience? What of the role of experience and experiences in fieldwork, given the contingences coursing through life and even more through fieldwork (if only we would see it), as with William Burroughs in 1965 telling *Paris Review*'s Conrad Knickerbocker what he sees at stake with his cut-up method (imagine him as an anthropologist, a subject he briefly studied, he says, as a graduate student at Harvard):

> I was sitting in a lunchroom in New York having my doughnuts and coffee. I was thinking that one does feel a little boxed in New York, like living in a series of boxes. I looked out the window and there was this great big Yale [mover's] truck. That's cut-up—a juxtaposition of what's happening and what you're thinking of. I make this a practice when I walk down the street. I'll say, when I got to here I saw that sign; I was thinking

this, and when I return to the house I'll type this up. Some of this material I use and some I don't. I literally have thousands of pages of notes here, raw, and I keep a diary as well. In a sense it's traveling in time.

Most people don't see what's going on around them. That's my principal message to writers: for God's sake, keep your *eyes* open. Notice what's going on around you.[2]

Being "subjective" like this implies being extremely "objective" and alert—indeed hyperalert. Keep your eyes *open*.

Then there is the question of time that automatically lends to the fieldwork diary a cut-up character. We see this vividly with the juxtaposition Burroughs presents of what is happening, put side by side with what you are thinking. More generally a diary eschews theory and entails an order of time that lies outside of narrative time structured by a beginning, middle, and an end. Precisely because its order is as remorseless as the rising and the setting of the sun, the diary frees up things. Or else it contains sporadic entries "when the moment seizes you," which form a daisy chain.

A diary is anarchic as regards the supposed laws of history. We construct a chronology of events. But we leave open the question as to what it is that connects those events. Later on someone with a low degree of tolerance for uncertainty may tie them together so as to construct the one big picture, but that's not the genius of the diary form, which maintains a wily tension between order and disorder, as does social life itself and all that's important.

What is more, time in a fieldworker's diary is oddly recursive. It moves ahead like a train, day by day or one entry to the next—that's for sure—but when we read and reread our diary, we are bound to another time that, like Proust's *memoire involontaire*, unexpectedly opens onto new worlds when two slabs of time, two quite separate moments of time, are for one reason or another juxtaposed. What makes a fieldwork diary unique is its property of combining these distinct types of time, the forward propulsion of day-succeeding-day chronology, combined with the sudden back-looping of connections that come about with reading and rereading the diary entries. A diary is certainly not an inert entity. It is a slumbering repository awaiting the lightning glance of its rereading, like the hibernating bear that one fine day in spring will awake with a start to a faster and larger rhythm of life. This back-looping is by no means a smooth ride. It is more a staccato of connections made abruptly between different times, plus a back and forth between action and its afterthought. Let me explain.

We so often act without knowing why. Later we cast a backward glance and look for a reason. Events beg for commentary, if not judgment. Your fieldwork notebook or diary is likely to bring forth and hold both these moments suspended in tension-filled antitheses.

These recursive movements of afterthought are themselves, I believe, the result of what Walter Benjamin claims to be the collector's deepest desire—to renew the old world—a desire that can be achieved by taking something from one context and adding it to another, such as the story of the devil in the cane fields of western Colombia, added by me to what I take to be capitalist commonsense in advanced economies where assumptions about the market suddenly seem strange when held up to the mirror of supernatural ideas involving the Prince of Darkness.

However, it is not only that the old world—my world before I got to the cane fields of western Colombia—has become renewed but that it has become seen by me and therefore, I hope, by my readers in a fundamentally new and enthralling way. That of course can amount to a renewal because this new way of seeing is the beginning of a new way of understanding one's understanding. This strikes me as something more powerful than a new or different idea. It is a communication from "the other side." It is a gift to the "old world," medicine for rethinking reality, more than an idea because it tears away at the edifice of thought and assumptions that allowed me to navigate my world until then. It has this wonderfully enlivening destructive quality. It is not—most definitely not—accumulation or part of one of those endearing upward "learning curves" I first heard about in the USA. Nor is it part of "learning from one's mistakes." Rather it is to begin the labor of cosmogenesis all over again from a different starting point.

The quality of new thought differs in other ways as well. It is highly physical, and theatrical. It is something that happened and continues to happen in your language and memories involving real people talking about other people in situ in the heat of the fields, the waving of the hands, the confidential tone, the clanging of pots and pans, the mystery and the banality and the dust and the deftness.

As I said, it is not so much a fact as a story, and not only a story but a gift to the "old world" that, like all gifts, demands a return. The devil story is actually a story told to capitalism, which initiated the conditions of its telling, awaiting the outsider in the shape of myself, a young, ignorant, bighearted galumph, to hand it over to a wider audience.

There is another gift-giving as well, working in the opposite direction, as with the account of local history focused on the immediate postslavery period after 1851 that Anna Rubbo and I published in 1975 in Spanish in Colombia for an audience largely of landless laborers and peasants in the area of fieldwork.[3] Based on oral history as well as luck in the state archive in Popayán, then under the directorship of don Diego Castrillón de Arboleda—descendant of one of the largest slave-owning families—the second half of the nineteenth century was excavated, that being the time when a free, prosperous, and rambunctious ex-slave peasantry existed along the rivers, free of state and landlord control, so very different to the appalling situation developing apace in 1975.

Gift meets gift. A circle. The insiders tell the outsider of the devil in the cane fields, and the outsider sees capitalist reality differently from then on. Then the outsider tells the insiders the stirring tale of the nineteenth century. Thus in both directions, moving out and moving in, a process of renewal was set into motion.

This certainly speaks to what (some) anthropologists do, because the "field," as in "fieldwork," is actually a meeting place of worlds, an interzone consisting of fieldworker and field creating therein a collage or intertext. The anthropologist is not presenting a picture of another reality so much as inhabiting a switchback by which one reality is pictured in terms of the other, which, in turn, provides a picture of that which pictures it!

So, what about *drawings* in a fieldwork diary? Are they the pauses, the occasional moments of still life where the writing hesitates between documentation and meditation? Are they the pauses connected to those moments when Proust's *memoire involontaire* unexpectedly opens onto new worlds when two slabs of time, two quite separate moments of time, are for one reason or another juxtaposed? Is that the privileged moment where words are likely to give way to images? If so, that would help explain the curious tension in the drawing *I Swear I Saw This*, an image caught in the recursive movement of time, first the words, then the drawing days later, such that words are converted into a caption as if all along they had been waiting to be completed that way.

Thus the drawing stands in contrast to a symbol, which is an image so perfectly adjusted to time that it becomes timeless and is appreciated on that count. But images that inhabit time—the recursive time of rereading—are historical, in a peculiar way. Being recursive, they flow with time yet also arrest it. Action and its afterthought. They are allegories, punched out of time, waiting. The allegory is called "the state of emergency" in which history merges into setting. Chronology is grasped and analyzed in a spatial image, as with the tunnels and freeways of modernity, at once mythic and profane, to create what Walter Benjamin, thinking of the baroque, referred to as a "petrified, primordial landscape" that could be summed up not only in a death's head but by a man juggling fire at the stoplight, or a woman sewing a man into a bag by the mouth of a tunnel.[4]

6

In 1976 Brion Gysin spoke into Terry Wilson's squeaky tape recorder, recalling the method of composition used by his writer friend William Burroughs in the cold Paris spring of 1958 when *Naked Lunch* was coming together. Burroughs had brought a trunkload of pages over from Tangier and was going off heroin, a disturbing state at best. Because his pages were never numbered, Burroughs would thrash around "in an ectoplasmic cloud of smoke," whining "Am I an octopus" as he sorted "through shoals of typescript with all tentacles waving in the undersea atmosphere." At the same time he would rant through the roles of his favorite fictional characters, such as Dr. Benway and hundreds of others he did not have time to "ram through the typewriter."[1] Could the historical connection between the "routines" and cut-ups, theater and chance, be any clearer?

"It's part of the method of 'dowsing things out,'" continued Gysin, with Burroughs "sort of humming a little tune (chuckling) with his mouth closed, and down his nose he's singing: *Yahe-e-e-pinta-a-a-r* (laughing)."[2]

Yagé pinta is the refrain you hear when taking the hallucinogen *yagé* with a Putumayo shaman in Colombia, as did Burroughs outside of Mocoa in 1953. It is like a command, "Paint *yagé*!" Or "Let the *yagé* paint!" But it is not the shaman singing so much as the *yagé* spirits themselves, singing through the shaman. What's more, the song is largely wordless—just what Burroughs and Gysin wanted, as expressed in their motto "Rub Out the Word." And here he is looking in his suitcase of pages of words for the pages and sequences of pages that will do just that while singing this song lifted out—should I say cut out?—of the rain-forested foothills of the Andes, a long way from room 25 or room 15 in the Beat Hotel.

"And this," continues Gysin, "the piece that he was looking for—or, an *even better one*—he has drawn up out of the mess that presents itself—so he pins it down and there he's got his, his piece or his book eventually."[3] Thus the cut-up method was used on *Naked Lunch* without "the author's full awareness of the method he was using" and the "juxtaposition of the sections was determined by the order in which the material went to the printer."[4]

Yet there could be an enormous investment in precision as well, Pythagorean in its magical adherence to permutations and grids. Always but always it was the high-tension mix and standoff between chance and the iron laws of fate—precisely what goes into sorcery.

A scrapbook owes much to the play of chance in the dialectic of order and disorder and can be thought of as not only the visual performance of chance but as a tool of chance, provoking unexpected memories and furtive connections reaching into the unknown. "What a resource for research!" you say. And you are right. Close cousin to a West African diviner's cowries, tarot cards, or a diviner's wheel, the scrapbook page is an instrument of divination. It is a site where fate settles, similar to certain valleys, outcrops of stones, or mountain passes, said to be propitious places for consulting the gods.

Antonin Artaud felt this strongly as he passed weirdly shaped giant rocks on horseback to take peyote with the Tarahumara Indians in northern Mexico. That was in 1936 when he was trying to get off heroin, an occasion, according to Burroughs, when a person "is subject to the emotional excesses of a child or adolescent."[5] He should know.

"The land of the Tarahumara," Artaud famously begins, "is full of signs, shapes, and natural effigies which do not seem to be mere products of accident, as if the gods, whose presence here is everywhere felt, had wished to signify their powers through these strange signatures in which the human form is hunted down from every side."[6]

There are accidents so accidental they must be the work of the gods.

I myself have a heavy ochre-colored fossil that sits by my keyboard in upstate New York. It is the size of a clenched fist, with symmetrical grooving spiraling into one side. I found it by chance in the valley of Ráquira in the high mountains of Boyacá in Colombia many years ago. Elizabeth Reichel-Dolmatoff told me her father told her that

Barranca de Urique.

Carl Lumholtz, *Unknown Mexico* (London: Dover, 1987 [1902]), 1:145

before the Spanish invasion this valley was—as I recall—"shamanic."
If anyone knew, it would have been him. It certainly felt wonderful
being there in Ráquira, and now I have my own "scrapbook," my own
collage, consisting of these memories, this fossil, my keyboard, and,
beyond that, my desk and window opening onto the river rushing over
the rapids with the pines beyond, the blue louvered wooden shutter
banging open and shut against the window with the wind. Proust gave
a name to this wind opening and shutting. He called it the *memoire
involontaire*. But let us not be too seduced by the mysteries of memory
and the pastness of the past, for what this wind opens are new insights
into the nature of things.

A fieldworker's notebook has something of this banging-shutter action too, although we don't usually see it that way. What would happen
if we did? The materials in such a book are deliberately sought out, it is
true. They are the reward of hard labor, it is true. Yet much is owed to
chance as well. Not only does chance pervade the notebook, but certain moments of chance are formative of entire projects and paradigm
shifts. These we celebrate as "discoveries" like Columbus "discover-
ing" the New World on his way to what he thought was India. What
a discovery!

Carl Lumholtz, *Unknown Mexico* (London: Dover, 1987 [1902]), 1:159

In my own work, perhaps better thought of as my own life, I can think of discoveries like this that came about through chance. I think of the hard work I have done and even more of all the waiting and boredom as not exactly irrelevant but as nothing more than a necessary prelude for chance to show its hand. The way I see it, a plan of research is little more than an excuse for the real thing to come along, in much the same way as the anthropologist Victor Turner described the value of writing down kinship diagrams as largely an excuse to stop falling asleep on the job and provide a situation in which the real stuff got a chance to emerge.[7]

As for that real stuff, there is no doubt that contingency provokes eye-opening back and forth, as when Laura Bohannan was asked by some Tiv people in Nigeria to tell them a story in the rainy season, which is when people are cooped up in their homes, and so she proceeded to relate Shakespeare's *Hamlet*, which was what she was reading at the time.[8] What followed was remarkable. The curious listeners became inquisitors. Hearing *Hamlet* through Tiv understandings of ghosts, witchcraft, death, marriage, remarriage, and inheritance meant not only displacing a European point of view. It meant that through chance, being asked to tell this story of Hamlet, she stumbled onto the most marvelous manner of illuminating one society in terms of another. Each moment of misunderstanding—or should I say understanding— as regards witchcraft or remarriage, for example, was a fruitful moment of contingency, opening a universe.[9]

Standing back from the scene of the storytelling itself, let us not overlook the play of chance in bringing this about: the fact of the rainy season, when people sit around and drink beer and tell stories as the swamps rise; the fact that Laura Bohannan, born and raised in the United States, had been given a copy of *Hamlet* in Oxford to take to Africa by a snooty Brit who said that Americans could not understand Shakespeare; the fact that with the rains she spent time alone in her hut reading *Hamlet*; and most of all the fact that the elders demanded she tell them a story, seeing as how they had told her so many. We who come later and from far away can read all these facts as links in a chain of cause and effect in a deterministic universe. Such an intricate weave of events plied one on top of the other must be what we mean by "fate," yet fate seems far removed from the mechanical world of cause and effect, for "fate" implies mystery. Are we not forced to admit that the concatenation of events around this Hamlet was a chance operation, like throwing two sixes with dice?

"The field was, as it were, alive and always changing, there was always something new to be learnt," writes Daisy Tan in her PhD dissertation concerning her fieldwork in a farmer's market in inner-city London.[10] I take this remark as testimony not only to the chance effect, but to the life-endowing qualities of that effect. "The field was, as it were, alive . . ." Here "the field" rightfully assumes its fetish status—a thing, become alive and always changing—even more than the fieldwork notebook and thanks to the fieldwork notebook.

Could it be that of all the different factors that go into granting the field the life of a fetish, it is chance that is most crucial? There are countless instances of chance discoveries in her daily work behind the counter where she sells apples, strawberries, and gooseberries fresh from the farm in Kent, where they are picked by Polish immigrants who work cheap. It seems like wherever she turns, the unexpected throws her a curveball. Like William Seward Burroughs, her eyes are wide open.

So much for the play of chance in the minutiae of fieldwork, yet chance determines entire projects too. How many times is an anthropologist asked, Oh! Why did you go to Colombia, or Brazil, or Fiji, or the University of Glasgow hospital? And the answer is inevitably crazy and generally a good story, a story of chance.

In June 1966 a friend casually tossed the morning newspaper, *La Republica*, to Daniella Gandolfo in a café in Lima, Peru. She was in Lima, her hometown, as a graduate student in the anthropology program of Columbia University, New York, to carry out research on the history of the city of Lima. On the front page was a photograph of a middle-aged woman street cleaner who had taken off her blouse to reveal her breasts when confronting the police in a workers' rights demonstration. The police backed off.

On seeing this photograph by chance, Daniella writes: "Then, it was as if the entire course of Lima's 460-year history had been abruptly arrested in the street sweeper's image, turned inside out and eviscerated into a moment of the city's prehistory . . . In retrospect, the moment I laid eyes on the image of the street sweeper, the still forming idea I had for an ethnography of Lima took a drastic and irrevocable turn."[11] She also points out that the writing in the fieldwork diary is itself prone to chance, nay, it is the prized chance-catcher in worlds made of the unexpected.

And let's not even get started on the role of chance and accident in writing the book from the notebook. This is far too complex and subtle. Like fieldwork, no one can teach it or even describe the rough outlines. You pick up a stray book, open it, start to read, and bang! There is a launching pad. You stare out the window for ages or at the blank wall, and bang! There's another launching pad. Or else a stray remark overheard, a blurred reflection in a shop window, whatever, the sparks fly. Or they don't, as with the sludge called "writer's block," which resists all and every attempt at cure. I recall the story of M. N. Srinivas, who lost his fieldnotes to fire in Palo Alto, California, on April 24, 1970—there's the accident, there's the precise date containing it—so he went on to write a delightful book, *The Remembered Village*, pretty much from memory. Could he have written a book if his notes were intact? After all, he had taken twenty-three years to even get to the point where he was sitting down to write when his notes went up in flames. A strange story indeed. He had three copies of his notes on his desk. Why? Three! And the notes in question were not really the original notes. Those were back in Delhi, safe and sound. So what were these notes that went up in smoke? As I said, let's not even get started on the role of chance and accident in writing.

As for my own voyage of discovery, which began with something safe and dull, compiling maps and figures on the history of land tenure in the southern Cauca Valley in Colombia, I was later shook from stem to stern in 1971 by the cooks who took me out to the cane fields. Busy with their pots and pans, one let drop a stray remark from the corner of her mouth about contracts with the devil that some cane cutters were said to be making so as cut more cane and get more money, even though, as I found out later, this would render the land thus worked infertile and the money could be used to purchase only so-called luxury goods like butter or sunglasses. It could not be used to purchase anything deemed productive, such as a plot of land to cultivate or an animal to fatten for market. The land would not yield and the animal would die. But there were no such stories about peasants working their own land. In other words, the devil was active in selling what Marx called "labor-power" as a commodity, but was not active when one still had a claim to means of production, which in this situation meant land. What is more, the peasant plots, consisting of trees, were free of chemicals and irrigation and required little labor, while the plantations denuded the land, required heavy inputs of weedkillers, fertilizers, and pesticides, as well as irrigation and much labor until labor-saving machinery was imported with generous government subsidies for the vast estates. Thus these wages of the devil cast fascinating light on the meaning of money and of the new types of labor in relation to nature and indeed to life, to living forms and their reproduction, to what today we call ecology.

This chance remark by the cooks out in the cane fields completely upset my planned research or, better put, destroyed it only to resurrect it on a more original plane of thought, where Marx's idea of the fetish of commodities, largely neglected until then in the Enlgish-speaking world, came into play. I had found a new world.

Another chance remark—or was it fate?—occurred a year later when I was with two peasant union organizers, Alfredo Cortés and Luís Carlos Mina, both farmers themselves, descendants of slaves brought from Africa. On scrawny ponies we rode up a spur of the Cordillera Occidental in southern Colombia to ask Indian serfs if they would volunteer labor and lumber to construct a meeting hall for the newly created peasant union in the market town of Santander de Quilichao in the valley below (Quilichao is said to have been the local Indian name, which translated to "land of gold"). To do this we had first to get permission from their *patrón*, a hardworking wiry guy named Zuñiga who, sizing me up, a young stranger with a medical degree and interested in history, started to tell me of the worrying illness from which he suffered—stomach pains and insomnia—which drove him to travel by bus way south along the *cordillera* past the colonial city of Popayán, through the baking hot Patía Valley, up along the cold mountains to the gray whispering city of Pasto not far from the border with Ecuador, stay the night, then take another bus snaking its way down the hairpin bends of the almost vertical mountainsides to the forests of the lowlands, where he would stay a week or longer with an Indian who would heal him using hallucinogenic medicines. Only later in discussion with Cortés and Mina on our return trip down the mountain, feet braced in the stirrups, did I realize that this illness was thought to be due to sorcery, something about which at that time I knew nothing.

A week later, in the market town, talking with some of his serfs who had a few drinks under their belts, I asked, "The *patrón* thinks he's ensorcelled. Who would be doing that?" With a grin lighting up his face and those of his companions, one responded, "Why! *Los mismos compadres!*" (*Why! His very own serfs!*)

A universe fell into my lap. There was no pressing reason for me to have gone up the *cordillera* with Cortés and Mina. I was Mina's friend. We did things together (and still do, forty years later). I was mad eager for the peasant's union to succeed, but that was not a reason to join them on this trip. It was more like I had time to kill and, as a resident of the monotonous flatlands of the valley, I was envious of those mountains. I so wanted to climb up there and lose myself in their blue haze. Moreover it was sheer accident that Zuñiga and I had gotten into conversation and that he had divulged the story of his journeys to the "ends of the earth" to seek a cure and spiritual armor from an Indian in the forest, and—here's the rub, as I was now hearing from my accidental encounter with the serfs in the crowded market—he was doing this so that he could withstand the sorcery he feared that his serfs, out of envy, were using to kill him. He was doing this so that he could continue to keep on top of them. But by the same token, so long as he imagined they had the power to ensorcell him, did not they, too, have power? The wheel kept turning over and over again. Zuñiga could keep on exploiting his serfs only so long as he had recourse to those other, supposedly more magically powerful Indians far away in the forested foothills of the Andes stretching into the Amazon basin. It was all in everybody's imagination, this magical expression of class warfare in the high Andes, and it made the role of that mind-bending medicine, whose name I later found to be *yagé*, to be of irresistible interest. I too had to go to the "ends of the earth" to experience this strange drug and talk with the medicine men who administered it. I had stumbled into a recapitulation of the forces unleashed by the Spanish conquest, with its attributions of magical power to the subaltern castes of Indians and African slaves, constituting today a webwork of magic spread across the land, encompassing high mountains, valleys, the Amazonian forests on the eastern escarpments of the Andes, and the sugarcane plantations in the interior. The healing journey of Zuñiga gives vivid expression to the ripple of deferral along a chain of racial fantasies, opening the Marxist chestnut of "class consciousness" to broader understandings of history's strange machinations as well as those of the human soul. And of course there are my own journeys to contend with as well.

Thanks to chance I had hit upon ideas and practices way beyond anything I could have imagined reading books in the reading room of the British Museum, where Marx had labored, or talking to my long-haired revolutionary friends in London, who no doubt would be called terrorists today. It was a moment of discovery made all the more poignant because it seems to confront head-on everything that is strange about chance itself. Let me put it this way. Among the persons I have just mentioned, such as Zúñiga and his serfs, and to a lesser extent Mina and Cortés, when something strange happens, especially something bad, chances are it is because of *sorcery*. Regularities are not the result of sorcery, but chance events are. Regularities pertain to *things of God*. Sorcery pertains to *cosas hechas, things done*, meaning "manmade," being a heavy-tongued euphemism not only for sorcery, known as the *maleficium* or *maleficio*, but also indicative of just how dependent on euphemism and indirection that world of sorcery is. (In the bureaucratic English-speaking secular world today, weird and terrible accidents are sometimes referred to as "acts of god," and not as sorcery, as when the limb of a tree in Central Park, New York City, fell and killed a child in 2010. Believe it or not, this is a secular, legal term meant to absolve human beings from any crime, to my mind thus shifting the event from sorcery to God.)[12]

The sorcerer then is the embodiment not only of chance but of free will in a world otherwise regulated by the god(s). But the gods are notorious for their willfulness too. Read *The Iliad*. Nietzsche has an idea. He tells us that "There must never be lack of real novelty . . . The course of a completely deterministic world would have been predictable for the gods and they would have grown quickly weary of it—reason enough for those *friends of the gods*, the philosophers, not to inflict such a deterministic world on their gods."[13] Hence in Colombia, to use Burroughs's terminology in the book he dedicated to Brion Gysin, the Magical Universe is pitted against that of the One-God Universe.[14]

Could we surmise, then, along with Burroughs and Gysin, that the world of sorcery is close to the play of chance as we find it in fieldwork notebooks and in scrapbooks? Even the same?

Well, yes, and no! Yes, in that sorcery certainly puts the emphasis on the untoward, and the un-to-ward is very much the snakelike action of chance in an unpredictable field. But no, in that from the sorcery point of view there can be no such thing as pure chance. To talk sorcery talk, to allege and diagnose sorcery, is to put order into disorder and make a claim for a world in which there is no such thing as a chance event. The world of sorcery is an overdetermined universe. Even chance, when you track it down, turns out not to be chance but the result of deliberation, meaning the sorcerer's machination. Back to my reflection on Artaud's journey to the land of the Taramuhara, and back to the limb falling on the child in Central Park: *there are accidents so accidental they must be the work of the gods.*

So where do we end up? What seems like chance, as opposed to order and system, turns out to fold itself back into the determined universe— but then this determined universe is more magical than magic!

This is the most disturbing thing about the play of chance destabilizing projects and making room for marvelous new ones. Like sorcery, chance entails fate, two sides of the one coin. This is why the diviner's wheel that is the scrapbook invokes not only magic but fate. This seems to me to be the same as the play of faith and skepticism in magic, including sorcery, and I dare say in religion too. It is a wonderful paradox that faith is at every step dogged by skepticism without which it cannot be. Hearken to E. E. Evans-Pritchard writing about the Azande people of central Africa in 1937: "Indeed, skepticism is included in the pattern of belief in witch doctors. Faith and skepticism are alike traditional."[15] Inseparable from this mix of faith and skepticism is the human body as the great stage of operations on which misfortune and cure unfold. In a zigzag pattern traced back and forth between faith and skepticism, revelation and concealment, the mystery is revealed, only to become still more mysterious.[16]

This same shell game is present in the play of chance and fate in a scrapbook and in a fieldwork notebook—and it must be why I am drawn to the action of enclosure and disclosure in the drawing I made of the bodies by the freeway, of the woman, if she is a woman, sewing the man, if he is a man, into a nylon bag. Her gesture goes further. She seems to be sewing herself into the same bag she is sewing him into. The walls of the freeway enclose her and they enclose me too as I am sped into the tunnel in a telescoping series of encysted enclosings that test and tease the figure-eight circuitry binding these bodies into traceries of revelation and concealment. The drawing is not the product of chance, but of chance as the underside of fate.

7

Had I unwittingly created a magical talisman, what those French surrealists such as George Bataille and Michel Leiris would call "sacred"?[1] What bravura! A bad drawing in a fieldwork notebook? How could that qualify for something as profound as "the sacred"?

Taking exception to the idea that the Lascaux cave paintings were made for utilitarian reasons, such as to ensure success in the hunt, Georges Bataille asserts his surrealist pedigree in suggesting instead that the paintings access *the marvelous* in homage to something awe inspiring and "hot," bearing on the spiritual kinship between people and the deer, bison, horses, and birds depicted. This would by no means exclude the desire to kill or capture such animals, but that desire is woven into a relationship with nature and spirits in which trapping, killing, respect, and what we could call worship are one. Think of the Naskapi hunters in Newfoundland, for instance, as recorded in the 1920s by Frank Speck. When they killed an animal they would stretch it out on its back, lay a carrying sling on it, put tobacco in the animal's mouth, and sit by it, smoking, for an hour or so. The animal, so we are told by Speck, who is himself not immune to serving up utilitarian explanations, is honored in this way, its reincarnation abetted, and the spirit master of the animals reconciled. Sometimes the hunter would sing and dance around the body of the animal as well.[2] This gets us close to John Berger drawing the face of his dead father, bringing it back to life, this same Berger who claims there is a deep kinship between drawing, song, and dance.

So here's a thought. Can we think of my drawing of the people by the mouth of the tunnel in this way too, as part of a barely conscious ritual—accidental, awkward, and solitary—that similarly strives to bear witness to the marvelous and bears a sacred charge? In our secular age, unlike Speck's Naskapi, most of us are not likely to be aware of such a charge and lack the language appropriate to it, wading clumsily through the sterile semantics of modern psychology or a rhapsodic romanticism. Nor have we thought overmuch about the meaning of bearing witness. But like a fish leaping unexpectedly out of the sea, the image provides testimony to the need to offer testimony.

My drawing is motivated by a sense of wonder, by Bataille's "marvelous," same as the "marvelously real" that the Cuban writer Alejo Carpentier waved provocatively in front of the Parisian surrealists as the real deal, drawn from the magical traditions manifest in the slums and poverty-stricken countryside of Haiti, although Carpentier failed to mention the poverty.[3] For sure my drawing is an exclamation of surprise too, inspired by the "marvelous-real," homage to a little bit of everyday hell.

And just as surely my drawing owes a good deal to the power of "sympathetic magic" set forth by Sir George James Frazer in a specific chapter in *The Golden Bough* concerning images found on magical charms in the ancient world and in the modern European colonies. It was Frazer's contention that in making an image for magical purposes, the idea is that what is done to the image will be replicated in real life. Hence the "sympathy." Actually this concept underlay his great work as a whole, purporting to explain the Dying God from Dionysus to Jesus as a mighty sympathy—a mighty magic—in synch with the passage of the seasons and hence with the crops and vegetation passing from the death of winter to the resurrection of spring. Yet despite his love of embellishment and fancy language, Frazer's host of examples running over one hundred pages in the chapter on charms have little magic to them since he treats magic as an idea-based activity and not as ritual, which, instead of being based on ideas and their logic, is based on action, atmospheres, and all that goes into the mise-en-scène of theater, including the subtleties of light and sound, as Artaud instructs. Frazer thus fails and fails miserably to get "inside" the reality of the magic, especially the emotional reality, and treats the "sympathy" more like a business negotiation, which is what drove Ludwig Wittgenstein mad in his blistering critique of what he identified as

Frazer's pointedly utilitarian view of magic as well as Frazer's assumption that we moderns neither possess nor need magic ourselves.[4]

In the opening pages of the extraordinary book *Pedro Paramo*, written in the early 1950s by the Mexican Juan Rulfo, we early on find the young narrator, fingering a dog-eared photograph of his recently deceased mother, who has sent him on a journey to hell, although he doesn't know that is where he's headed just yet.[5] Instead he is walking in the heat with a mule driver through a barren, mountainous landscape in search of his father's village, but once he gets there, as through an invisible portal, he will, without at first realizing it, enter the land of the dead and the horrors with which they are associated. As he touches the photograph of his mother prior to entering the village, conscious of carrying out her last wishes and recalling her antipathy toward being photographed because a photograph is so useful to sorcery, he feels that the image is sweating, just as he is sweating. The image is full of needle holes and over the heart (*corazón*) there is one big hole—big enough to fit the middle finger (finger de *corazón*). And it is this image he intends to show his father, whom he has not seen since childhood and who, unbeknownst to him, is long since dead.

Fingering the hole-strewn photograph is the key moment taking us from the ordinary to the extraordinary world. We readers too will now enter into that hole through the heart in the image. In the case of my drawing, that heart is the cocoon into which the woman on the freeway by the tunnel is sewing the man.

There was no need, in my opinion, for Frazer to so determinedly yoke the magical power of mimicry to utility. It seems to me true, wonderful, and troubling that if you imitate something, you enter into its orbit and exchange something of its being with your own. But we cannot, and must not, attribute such magical thinking or what Freud called the belief in the omnipotence of thought to so-called primitive people but not to ourselves. Indeed, such an attribution is but an all too typical colonial example of projecting onto others what we want but dare not utter, what we truly believe, but must not. We have our taboos, too.

I myself cannot not believe in this sympathetic magic of mimicry. But it seems like every age brings forth new words to describe it. Or avoid it. Why is that? When I write I nearly always have this feeling of entering into what I am writing about. To read writing that circles around images makes this feeling even stronger—as with Juan Rulfo's image of the hole in the mother's heart through which one's heart finger can pass so as to enter the Other world. But it's only an image, an image of an image.

So what might mimesis have to do with my drawing of the people by the tunnel and hence with witnessing? Is the drawing magical in terms of Frazer's sympathetic magic, and if so, to what end? Surely it cannot be for a desire to have that which is depicted enter into the life of the artist? Is it perhaps like the picture with the hole in the *corazón*, through which we might enter into an enchanted world? Is it sacred in the sense of Bataille's idea of recognizing the marvelous? Or is there perhaps an additional idea at work here to which these contrasting and complementary positions might point us?

For a long time I wanted to say that shock is the critical element here, and my reasoning went like this. My shock at seeing people lying by the tunnel required, consciously or unconsciously, an image that could be thought of as a way of absorbing the shock so as to get control over it, and here Frazer's utilitarian approach to the sympathetic magic of mimesis comes to mind. Yet on top of that Frazer effect there exists the homage to the marvelous, providing the ritual setting—albeit in a notebook—in which a little bit of everyday hell is given its due. Putting all this together amounts to *witnessing*.

What is important here is the sacred quality of horror. Not stained-glass windows or rapturous images of saints. Rather their ruin. In the regions from which I report, this is everyday and everyday worse.

The real shock—if that is the word—now seems to me to be that we so easily accept scenes like the one of the people by the tunnel. In the blink of an eye they pass into oblivion. The real shock is their passing from horror to banality. The real shock is that fleeting moment of awareness as to the normality of the abnormal, which, as with a wound, soon covers itself over with scar tissue. "Why do they choose this place?" I asked the driver. "Because it's warm in the tunnel," he replies. To witness, therefore, is that which refuses, if only for an instant, to blink an eye.

8

This everydayness of the monstrous—not the monstrous itself—is a complicated state of being that comes easily unstuck. Instead of a gradual process whereby we adapt to the weird and the horrific and treat it as normal, the normality of the abnormal is a tensed combination of opposites, a split consciousness that unexpectedly veers off into scary territory when you least expect it, such as when, for whatever strange concatenation of events, abject life hurls itself at you, and in wild disbelief you can only exclaim: *I Swear I Saw This.*

Why swear?

Is it to emphasize the unruly unbelievability of the sighting? Is it to emphasize that to witness is not just to have your eyes open at the right spot at the right time? What, after all, is the difference between *seeing* and *witnessing.* If I say that my drawing is an act of witness, what I mean to say is that it aspires to a certain gravity beyond the act of seeing with one's own eyes. To *witness,* as opposed to *see,* is to be implicated in a process of judgment—even if the court before which one is called to bear witness is (how shall I put this?) imaginary, such that the mere act of seeing tilts the cosmos and deranges the eyeball. How shall I put this? The staid and stable act of perception separating a subject, like a lookout tower, from an object, like a specimen, founders. The *who am I?* and the *what is that?* gets messed up because the field implicating observer and observed has suddenly become a zone of trench warfare, putting extreme pressure on language—as opposed, say, to a drawing.

Why can't language alone serve as testimony here? Why the drawing? Is there some inevitable primitivism here that sidesteps language, as when for example I invoke Lascaux and the Naskapi, and John Berger lumps together drawing, singing, and dance—our corporeal gang? And you might say, "Well, as a matter of fact, there is language. Look at the writing, *I Swear I Saw This.*" But then I can respond and say to you that it's incantatory. That it's at least halfway to poetry, language with a difference, language halfway to wordless song, as with Burroughs singing *yagé pinta* while he rifles through the scattered pages of writing in his suitcase. Is that primitivism too?

In thinking about the split consciousness of the normality of the abnormal, of the monstrous as an everyday part of everyday life, in Colombia, if not elsewhere, I am mindful of the everydayness of the miracle. For the miracle is by definition spectacularly unusual. Yet for people who—as we say—"believe in miracles," such as the majority of the poor country people I know in Colombia, they are also part of life.

The miracle may be statistically rare, but it is not that which makes it normally abnormal and vice versa. Rather it is the sudden intrusion of the Other world into our mundane world that is here at issue. This same stroke of fate, this same tear in the fabric of reality, was set forth by Walter Benjamin in his essay on surrealism in which, in an attempt to curb the "New Age" type of occultism that he saw as tempting surrealism in the 1920s, he wrote of the need for a "dialectical optic" that perceives the "everyday as impenetrable, the impenetrable as everyday."[1]

To what degree this handy formula frees us of the occult is questionable, for surely it is there hovering in the wings—as with *retablos* and *ex-votos*, these being paintings or small sculptures of body parts like arms or eyes or breasts made in Latin America that *testify to a miracle* like surviving an earthquake, being in a bus falling over a cliff, or incurring a fatal disease. As with Bataille's suggestion regarding the Lascaux cave drawings, they come *after* the miracle. They give "voice" to the marvelous.

In the paintings, the scene is crudely drawn. An angel or saint may be pictured in the sky. A text within the frame explains the miraculous salvation, and the resulting artwork is then hung in the church. All of which is pretty much what I have done in my notebook—the notebook of course being the equivalent of the church, which presents us with yet another paradox parallel to that of the miracle and of the normality of the abnormal, the notebook being a work tool, yet something else as well.

It is not surprising then that Bataille puts play in the realm of the sacred, as when he writes with regard to the Lascaux cave paintings that "the fullness and reality of the game man plays are consequences of his overstepping what is prohibited."[2] And that is how I regard drawings such as mine in my notebook—as *play*, to be contrasted with the text, which is *work*. Such drawings have no place in the anthropologists' canon. They are fun to do. They overstep. You are not meant to make silly drawings, let alone smoke and dance over the corpse. They are marginal at best, a retreat to childhood and therefore—from the perspective of Bataille—not merely products of caprice and innocence, but likely to be deadly serious and in fact more serious—more sacred—than work could ever be.

Talking of miracles is pretty easy. There is a well-trodden path laid out for us. But what of the miracle that is, so to speak, *negative*, what the Bataille-Kristeva crowd refers to as "abject horror" and such like, meaning yuck + fear, served up with attraction + repulsion? For, cringing in my abjectivity, this is how I think of the scene by the freeway and of my obsession with it. As opposed to *object*, or *subject*, the *abject is* meant to suggest a bit of each *glued together*! I am stuck in the no-man's-land of the people by the tunnel. Their space has become mine, and I am neither myself any more, nor am I an object.

And if it is perplexing to experience such a state, it is stranger still to express it—because the task is not only to express that which is, but also that which is not: what Bataille at one point described as "the apex of a thought whose *end* jumps the rails on which it is travelling."[3] In other words, the incredulity of *I Swear I Saw This*.

In modern courts of law, to swear the oath is the rite that guarantees truth, whether this oath be taken on a holy book or not. To *swear* is that which stands outside truth so as to ensure it. To *swear* represents an Other source of truth that the factual truth requires. For years George W. Bush's White House aides refused to testify under oath to the U.S. Senate Judiciary Committee as part of its investigation into the politicization of the Justice Department under Alberto Gonzales. To lie under oath is a criminal offense. The aides were prepared to testify, but not under oath. And this in our grandly secular age! The aides would not declare *I Swear I Saw This*. They strenuously refused, and this had the makings of a huge fight about executive privilege.

But to *swear* also means to utter bad language, foul language that bears the potential to magically hurt the person, thing, or event at whom or at which it is directed. This was the earlier meaning of the *curse* as magically empowered, flipside of the *oath*.

In his book on free slaves from the United States escaped to Canada, Brion Gysin describes the animosity of Irish migrants toward the blacks in the 1830s. Schools had been set up for Negro children by Laura Haviland, who had to pass by the shanties of the Irish, who would curse her. "And a most thorough business of it they made," she says, "beginning with the ground I walked on, they would curse the nails of my shoes and their laces, enumerating every article I wore and ending with my immortal soul and the hair on my head."[4]

How these two meanings combine—the truth swear and the cursing swear—how they partake of the same magical power is a puzzle, something we perform every day without a thought. Perhaps it goes like this, that to lie under oath about one's witnessing would be to have the swearing turn on the swearer as curse? All this reposes deep in our language, older times and older beliefs embedded in current ways. "A whole mythology is deposited in our language."[5]

Yet what I mean by the power of witnessing is outside of any court of law. The witnessing effect I have in mind—as with my drawing of the people by the tunnel—is somehow naked, shorn of support other than itself.

Okay, what does this mean, "shorn of support other than itself"? To whom or what are you swearing when you write "*I Swear I Saw This*"? That is the fundamental question.

9

To whom are you writing?

Around 1995 in a sugar plantation town in Colombia, I tried to heal someone from sorcery. My patient, whom I had known since she was three years old, was the adorably eccentric seventeen-year-old daughter of a cane cutter who had migrated to this town from the jungles of the far-off Chocó adjoining Panama in the 1960s, and subsequently left on his own for Venezuela around 1980. Over the past six months the girl had grown listless, stopped eating, and nothing could shake her out of her despondency. Her mother was frantic, fearing that a neighbor had bewitched her as revenge, the neighbor being of the opinion that the mother had killed her daughter by magical means in childbirth.

Faltering in self-confidence as I sang over my patient, I found myself drifting in my mind over the mountains down into the foothills on the Amazon side of the Andes, where, for two to four weeks, year after year for three decades, I had accompanied my friend Santiago Mutumabjoy as he cured people of sorcery with his singing and hallucinogenic medicine. In a manner never made clear to me, this curing involved spirits such as the spirits of the medicine, the spirits of the forest, and the spirits of the river.

I heard my singing tremble, and felt my self-confidence drain away. I thought to myself that in order to keep singing and pull this off I would have to be able to conjure these spirits too, or if not them at least the people far away on the other side of the mountains in the forest who, as far as I can tell, do believe in spirits. So I sang and envisioned, in my mind's eye, at least, and was able to finish what I had set out to do. Did the spirits ensure the song, or was it the song that brought the spirits into being?

Much later, in 2008, an undergraduate student at Columbia University, Celine Sparrow, told me that when she sings with her a capella group she finds that she imagines an object or a scene. Does the image precede the sound, or vice versa? She is not sure. The crucial thing is that that image and sound interact so that the body of the singer synchronizes with the song and the sound is given a body. For a series of *la la las* in one song, she imagines a sailboat on the ocean. The waves become increasingly turbulent, then calm down. For another song, about war in Ireland, one image that comes to her concerns the content, and another image concerns the sound. For the bass notes, which is what she sings, *doom dee da deedee doom dee da da*, she sees in her mind the footsteps of the soldiers on an empty battlefield after bloody combat. True to her name, Sparrow signed off her email with a "tweet."[1]

Such imaging seems to me and to her to be a way of allowing the body to carry out complex maneuvers unconsciously. What I call the "bodily unconscious" requires a critical degree of consciousness, but not too much, as that would derange the finely calibrated autonomicity of the body—breathing, shape of the soft palate, positioning of the vocal cords, tone of the sound, rhythm, timing, and so on.[2]

Here's the crux: it is the image that allows the body to be straddled by a barely conscious consciousness. And that is a small—everyday—miracle. One that provides the song with a body. This seems to me to shed light on spirits as much as on my drawing of the people by the tunnel.

When I sang my curing song, I had dodged the question as to whether spirits exist by substituting real people for them in my imagination, real people who do believe or seem to believe in them, but for whom I suspect they remain nevertheless more half-real than real, if I may put it this way, just as do Sparrow's images. The spirits may actually be seen by my friends of the forest—indigenous or poor colonists—when taking hallucinogens in sorcery-laden atmospheres, but then a lot of other strange things are seen as well, quite apart from spirits, and under these conditions seeing is not like it used to be anyway.

Seeing here is special. More like *witnessing*. What is more, seeing here cannot be separated from singing and is inherently world-changing as well. Spirits thus seem more like ways of touching the ineffable edge to life and more like storytelling than discrete things in themselves, just as singing casts a shadow quite different to speaking.

When I had finished and gone back to where I was staying, I tried, days later, to write about this in my fieldwork diary, but it was difficult. I found myself struggling with the questions about what a diary is and to whom one is writing when one writes in a diary, and I found I had to discard the obvious answers as self-deceptive. For example, you do not "write for yourself" because there is always a bigger "you" than yourself, a "you" of many readers looking over your shoulder. Or else the "you" has become quite another you, in fact many versions of yourself shifting around like lost souls desperate for a warm body. And it is just as obvious that this other audience, this invisible, ephemeral, audience looking over your shoulder as "you" write, is there in every writer's imagination, no matter what they are writing, fiction or nonfiction or a fieldwork diary.

In this dilemma I hit upon a novel idea. Might not that invisible audience reading over your shoulder as you write in your notebook belong to that same phantom world of spirits I was singing to when trying to cure the young woman in the plantation town? Here was a happy coincidence indeed; precisely because I was having such a difficult time trying to write in my notebook about what had just transpired with spirits or spiritlike entities, I hit upon a solution to the question "For whom does one write?" The spirits! Yes! All writers are writing for the spirits, especially when writing a diary.

Of course, spirits can get in the way, too, as every writer knows when blocked and flummoxed due to spiritual bad temper or envy. Then the writer has to summon other spirits and all manner of tricks to deal with the roadblock. Sylvia Plath made it a habit to consult the *I Ching* before writing so as to minimize such blocks. Other writers go for a walk, make coffee, consult their email, whatever, or else perform elaborate preventive measures like those male writers who wear suits when writing and lock themselves away in the basement like hermits. I have seashells I picked up from the high-tide mark on the beach at Seal Rocks just north of Newcastle on the east coast of my native Australia that I place close to my keyboard, as well as a hefty fossil from Colombia and my hard-of-hearing cat named Norman. Gifted Cherokee dancers hold a mirror while dancing in order to ward off envious spirits, Jimmie Durham once told me, so perhaps I will add a mirror or two, because you can't be too careful.

In place of a person-to-person psychology, writing would seem to involve a writer-spirit-reader reality in which things—from the *I Ching* and tarot cards to seashells, fossils, and good old Norman himself—play the role of humanlike spirits, whom we writers use as much as we are used by. In my field, most writers use a spirit they call "theory," a very powerful spirit indeed, usually with a French or German name. But this can be dangerous, like a pact with the devil, and only practitioners experienced with such pacts should do this.

Sometimes the spirits such as Sparrow's boat sailing through the waves are one's assistants. I am not only singing *to* them but *with* them as my spirit helpers who then carry the song to its perfection across the waves, thereby allowing all manner of beings their freedom somewhere between the bodily unconscious and the bodily unconscious of the world. Other times they get in the way, but either way they are there dancing and implicated.

So this is my conclusion: could it be that when one belatedly scribbles in red pencil in one's diary *I Swear I Saw This* that one is actually conjuring spirits—just as I was doing when singing my curing song? And try this one too: might what I witnessed in Medellin be the spirits of modernity—spirits of the freeway, spirits of the dark tunnel, and the fire-dealing spirit of the crossroads?

This seems ridiculous and worse than sketchy, thus situating real people in desperate circumstance. Yet the equation endures, perhaps because in those very circumstances of dread and danger real people emanate a spiritlike character that affects us all. In which case, bearing witness, as with my sketch, is to hail these same spirits, an acknowledgment from a faceless passerby as to the charge they put into the world.

Or try this: it's not that they are spirits, half-real at best, but that they become spirits when traduced into a drawing in a fieldwork notebook, heartland of the fetish.

10

To cure, I invoked not spirits but pictures in my head of people that I believed believed in spirits. In my mind a whole movie was reeling out, here in the hot, treeless town of cramped little houses and marauding gangs surrounded by sugarcane plantations. But there, covered with blue haze, were the mountains, and as I got closer (in my mind, you understand) ruffled forests gave way to white cactus-like *frailejon* dotting the peat bogs of the cold *paramos* twelve-thousand-feet high on deserted plateaus. The path wound onward, tilting down steep slopes and ravines to pause at the faces of friends and acquaintances, Indians and poor colonists, men and women, leaning forward, faces, their faces, catching the light, faces of people far more at home with spirits than I was, and that was good enough for me to keep going with my wordless song. Me, a man out of his depth and off course, whichever way you look at it. Not a drawer. Not a singer. What good be such a man?

Spirits, pictures, and song. It is to this combination of spirit with image via song that I am drawn when I think about my picture of the woman sewing the man into the nylon bag by the freeway tunnel in Medellin. Being drawn to draw, equivalent to singing, is what makes the difference between *seeing* and *witnessing*.

I need to work this strangeness—this combination of spirit with image via song—into my understandings of drawing, recalling John Berger's notion that "drawing is as fundamental to the energy which makes us human as singing and dancing."[1] Drawing, he said, has something that painting, sculpture, videos, and installations, lack—corporeality.[2]

On this account, drawing integrates with particular power what Friedrich Nietzsche saw as distinct yet combined ways of being in the world. On one side we find that half-man, half-woman, that wine-sodden dancing stranger in our midst. This is the side of Dionysus, the lover of song and music and dance. On the other side, that of Apollo, god of form and boundaries, there is visual art, including sculpture. Dionysus wants us to live within the image and vice versa, have the image take us over, body first, such that the Self dissolves into a thousand selves that know little distinction between body and mind, conscious and unconscious, individual and collective. Apollo, however, wants distance. Apollo wants image, held at arm's length away from the body, a feast for the eyes but not the mouth, shoring up the enclosed and stable entity we today in the West call our Self.

The question, however, is whether what we call "image" as opposed to body, this realm of Apollo as opposed to Dionysus, can be so neatly delineated? While much can be said about this problem, what is important to me is what happens in the act of drawing or in the act of looking at a drawing and how that relates to thinking and acting in the world, for if drawing is corporeal, it must be the mediator par excellence between body and image, and looking at a drawing must have some of this as well.

Thanks to song and wine, the Dionysian character dissolves into the world to become its polymorphous magical substance imitating anything and everything for the sheer love of mimicry and love of mimetic excess. Through imitation such a being enters the body of another being, such that the world "has a coloring, a causality, and a velocity quite different from those of the world of the plastic artist and epic poet," writes Nietzsche in *The Birth of Tragedy*.[3]

But he then adds that this entering into bodies and hence into what I call the body of the world *is achieved by seeing oneself surrounded by images or something like images, which he calls spirits*—a "host of spirits"—such that hand in hand with the madness and the ecstasy there are visions.

In other words, it is true that Apollo might seem to limp behind lived experience so as to record it in pictures. Yet is he not busy in the very heart of the action, where images we call spirits surround us, where the visions come and go in the ex stasis of ecstasy? For the absolutely crucial thing is that Apollo provides the picture that the song needs so that the person off course can stay the course.

The interactive process between image and song that I am now equating with drawing must be stupendously relevant for the shamans I got to know in the Putumayo River basin of Colombia who drink a hallucinogen known as *yagé* and then dispense it to a small group of ensorcelled persons, singing a wordless song in stops and starts the night long. The interaction between image and song is especially relevant, because while the healer succumbs to the intense bodily experiences of the hallucinogenic medicine, dancing in and out of bodies, so to speak, dissolving selfhood, he remains "on top" with a critical consciousness so as to attend to the people being cured, many of whom are in desperate shape when the *yagé* takes full effect. It is my distinct impression, in fact, that the more desperate the situation, the more people are wasted and freaking out, the more the shaman drinks and the more he becomes intoxicated so as to handle the situation. At those times, the singing is likely to be ascendant and strong, fighting the tempest, and there may be fierce dancing, as I recall with four young Kofán shamans on the Guamuéz River in 2007 near Santa Rosa. In their rubber boots stamping on the raised, swaying floor of split planks, they were singing and dancing in unison, big men with huge shoulders like linebackers for Ohio State, crazy-sounding yet Oh! so gentle.

But it is not only image and song that thus interact along the edge of consciousness. For there is also what we could call the theater of exterior and interior spaces within which the image and song occur; a theater of fear, with its sense of stepping into the unknown, the personal dissolution, the staging with the copal incense burning, the flickering light and shadows leaping from a candle stuck by a dusty Catholic icon accompanied by nausea, vomiting, and shitting, giving way to floating calm, the body turning tricks on itself as images cascade and selves telescope out of other selves. In 1975 I wrote of my experience.

The candlelight creates shapes of a new world, animal forms and menacing. The lower half of my body disappears. I learn to use dissociation as an advantage, as a way of escaping the horror. I am not the person being got at; rather I am the disembodied face-presence calmly peering in and watching this other and unimportant me. I watch my other self, safely now. But then this second me, this objective and detached observer, succumbs too, and I have to dissociate into a third and then a fourth as the relation between my-selves breaks, creating an almost infinite series of fluttering mirrors of watching selves and feeling others.[4]

Were ever Dionysus and Apollo more at war with one another than here? Or more entwined? The struggle to maintain the self breaks apart, and then again and again in a world of strange creatures come from lands of fear and laughter larded with storytelling, dreams, and the shaman's song. Everything is porous. You yourself, reality, and the night itself, broken into countless stops and starts. Now and again the shaman plays a melody on an old mouth organ he got from someone in the U.S. Peace Corps. Other times someone with a lot of experience with *yagé* will start to hum too. The hammocks creak. The cold wind comes through the cracks in the plank walls. A dog stirs. At Salvador's place in 1975 deep in the forest by the Guamuéz River, tributary of the Putumayo, there was just a thatch roof without walls, and you could hear and almost see the monkeys high in the canopy of the forest as Salvador served each of us *yagé* by the glow of a small fire.

Can the image be separated out from this ephemera of flicker and shadow and the body gone mad? Can it be separated from the singing, the entire Dionysian conspiracy of medicines used to massage the body in the curing at dawn as the wind whips off the river in the valley below and the cocks crow? Let me not forget other medicines like *agua fresca* to calm someone freaking out, the brandy drunk, the alcohol rubbed on the body, and the brutal nettles of the fleshy *ortiga* plant whipped across the naked back raising welts when a person feels particularly beleaguered and pleads for this treatment.

And then there is the dying, passing through nausea and paranoia into the space of death, where the journey really begins and all sorts of possibilities—and disasters—may occur. This is present in the drawings that emerge from the *yagé* experience, like the *ex-votos* and *retablos* I mentioned earlier, bearing witness to the normal abnormal that is the miracle, that impenetrability of the everyday blended with the everydayness of the miracle.

When young Bosco drew for me the *yagé* vision that most appalled him, I was struck by the way he spoke as if *seeing* was *making real* in the midst of his fear of sorcery. At times his language seemed quite

The Sorcerer, by Juan Bosco

distorted, *seeing seeing*, sort of thing. But this language is accurate enough. Here is what this fourteen-year-old boy, son of a white peasant colonist, drew for me in an uninebriated state in the lowlands of the Putumayo region of Colombia around the small town of Mocoa in the early 1980s.

"Why do you take *yagé*?" I asked. And Bosco responded, saying you take *yagé* to see who is doing sorcery against you, to . . . clarify the situation, and *at the same time* (my emphasis) to cure yourself.

Seeing what is going on alters what's going on, at least in the *yagé*-inflected, sorcery-saturated world of being. The keyword used is *pinta*, as in *painting*, which I take to be the same as *witnessing*.

Bosco describes the *pinta* he drew at my request a year or so later:

I saw a man making what we call *brujerías* [sorcery] in our farm. He wanted to see all our cattle dead and us begging for alms. He wanted to see us like I was seeing. Later I saw my father, and his bad friends wanted to see him as a sorcerer like him. Then I saw my father in his underpants with a tail [like the devil] in the form of a chain, and his body naked. I saw that. The others said that was how they wanted to see him. And they laughed when they saw that I saw that. They said they wanted to take him away . . .

Later on Sister Carmela [a white spirit healer from the city of Pasto in the highlands] also said that the man I saw doing sorcery was the sorcerer. She hears that from the spirits, and with them she can cure. She calls the spirits . . . like Tomás Becerra [a dead Indian shaman of the Putumayo lowlands who was the first to give Bosco's father *yagé* to drink when he came as a youngster to the lowlands].

Later on taking *yagé*, I saw my father curing the farm. The drunkenness of the *yagé* caught me and took me there. I thought I was going to suffer too. Then I saw my father converting himself into a dove, and in the *yagé* I saw Sister Carmela and my uncle Antonio dressed in white cleaning the farm.[5]

The actual drawing he made for me has a striking form and is quite different from the narrative above. It can be seen as the storyboard for a movie that he related like this: the top left is of an evil highland Indian, the epitome of sorcery in the eyes of non-Indians; the top right presents Bosco's family farm with sorcery substance inside of a rotting tree stump; and the bottom left is of the sorcerer, a white man, holding in his hand the sorcery substance, *the capacho*, made of bones and dust found in the cemetery.

Then there is the casual, everyday way Bosco refers to spirits when he describes Sister Carmela conjuring spirits—such as the dead Indian shaman, Tomás Becerra—from whom she hears what is going on in the murky worlds of sorcery, betrayal, and the spirits of the dead.

Carmela once laid her shaking hands on my supine body in a darkened, second-story room in the mountains in the sad, quiet city of Pasto. Possessed by the spirit of a dead Venezuelan doctor, José Gregorio Hernández, speaking in a gruff male voice, she set about curing me. There was no song here, no hallucinogens, and no humor or storytelling. It was sheer belief and the unnerving energy of her trembling body. Yet she too combines Apollo and Dionysus, does she not? Her body is a firestorm of tremulousness. Dionysus vibrato. But it is the Apollonian accent on the image of the spirit of the dead that provides the trigger, first of the good doctor from Caracas, José Gregorio

Hernández, immaculate in his dark suit and homburg hat, and then of other spirits of dead healers, like the Indian shaman from the lowlands of the Putumayo, Tomás Becerra.

In Carmela's art, the image possesses her body so as to cure sick people. In Bosco's art of the image, he is both inside and outside the image, a moving image, at that. This enclosure in the image is what will allow—if this is your fear, if this is your aim—the image to change what it is an image of.

Then there is Bosco's father, a wiry peasant colonist who senses, like everyone else in the Putumayo, that he is surrounded by envious neighbors who are likely to ensorcell him. What he loves is to take *yagé* with his inseparable companion, one of the great Indian shamans whom he one day found collapsed and dying in his home. "You sing, don José, you sing," croaked the shaman. "Aren't you always singing and curing, hidden under your poncho in the dark when we take *yagé*?"

Okay, so I got busy with my medicines and then the *chuma* [the drunkenness of *yagé*] caught everyone and it was terrible! His son-in-law was crying, "Don José please come and cure me because I am dying." I bent over him and exorcised, cleaning and sweeping and sucking . . . and then I worked on don Santiago until three in the morning and then he began to revive, to speak again, "Ya ha ha," and he would whistle and scream . . . He also saw the cemetery, all of it. "Avé María," he said, "dead people putrefying everywhere," he said. Others in agony about to die. The whole house a graveyard. Avé María.[6]

Yagé inserts you into "the scene of the crime" as picture. There perhaps you can cure, which is what Bosco's father is trying to do in his mental picture, being put into the unexpected position of curing his mentor, an Indian shaman—such a personage being the very source of magical power as conceived of in longstanding colonial fantasy about Indians of the forest. Both men could see the graveyard beckoning. Bosco's father saved the situation, thanks to his ability to move into the picture. But for the Indian shaman, the power of *yagé* to open you to the world and move into image had proven destructive. The power of *yagé* that allows you to see and to heal as much as to sing, be wise, and play the fool, also makes you vulnerable to attacks by other shamans envious of your powers. That is why at times its gets to be too much. Then the *chuma* is overwhelming. Bosco's father continued:

> A terribly strong *chuma* caught me up. *Virgen Santisima!* I felt I was dying . . . what exhaustion, what terror! So much so that I had no idea what to do . . . I was on my farm [i.e., he could see a picture of his farm]. I knew who was doing this evil to me. At that moment I grabbed alcohol and my medicines and massaged myself with them. I wafted incense. I lit a cigar. I caught the incense. Its fragrance made me cough. I conjured it in the name of God. Thus one cures . . . And it was a pretty picture curing myself, no?[7]

Years after Bosco's father told me this story I took *yagé* with him and the shaman in question, Santiago Mutumbajoy. A couple of days later I made the following drawing in my notebook. They were both singing and beating time with their curing fans of dried leaves as I sat, so abject, rigid, and mute, on the floor between them. Their songs criss-crossed. Bosco's father's singing sounded like Catholic church music. It was melodic yet plaintive with high-pitched sadness. There was screeching and crying. I knew that his wife was slowly dying. Santiago's singing, on the other hand, was bold, somewhere between speech and the wind and the belly-shuddering frogs shaking the rain forest. As I looked up from where I was sitting on the floor, Bosco's father became all face, and the face changed from that of a white man to that of a stone statue I had seen in the mountains in San Augustín just north of here, made before Europeans came to the New World.

Was this one of the faces I saw years later when I was trying to cure the young woman in the town by the sugarcane fields and I conjured in my imagination people who believed in spirits? Like me, a white man transforming into a shaman, an Indian shaman, floating above us, a wild and desperate angel.

Bosco's sick mother, a white woman come down twenty years ago from the highlands, tremulous, cheeks drawn, paralysis setting in due to some mysterious illness, could barely speak. Sometimes she became possessed, she said, by the spirit of a young lover who died long ago in a truck crash. When he came, he sat on her right shoulder. In her querulous voice, she told me he looked like a *gringo*, and her gaze

A wild and desperate angel

settled uncomfortably on me. Not for her, the taking of *yagé* with Indians whom, by and large, she detested and feared. She invoked the spirit of Tomás Huamanga, whom she described as a Venezuelan who died 350 years ago. She was very precise and then she showed me a photograph of this spirit. What a surprise! It was a picture of a local Indian!

Subject to many generations of Xeroxing, this photograph now hovers, so it seems to me, midway between a photograph and a drawing. Indeed I find I cannot tell whether the "photograph" she put in my hand was not originally a drawing. How spooky the image is, as if repeated copying has brought out its spiritual power. With this eerie image, she has no need of *yagé*! Poised between photograph and drawing, the image itself creates a *yagé* effect. If ever I had to make an image of a spirit, this would be it. No need for spirit photography. Just the

Bosco's mother's image (Rosario's image)

Xerox machine and life at the edge of the jungle. Again and again, copies of copies, until the flat image becomes something ethereal, looking more like some exotic fruit about to peel off its many strands of being. And if we could see succeeding generations of copies made after this one, they would give way to intimations of substance, like the dust of dirt and bones in the cemetery awaiting a sorcerer to make a *capacho* like the one you see in the hands of the sorcerer in Bosco's drawing, lower-left side.

The face of the Indian in Bosco's mother's photograph is solemn and determined. What is being looked at so fixedly? Something we cannot see. It must be of the same light and shadow that condenses on the face, striations of darkness caught briefly on the bead necklace and on a solitary plantain leaf, wide and luscious, in the background.

Not only is this woman dying, but worse than dying, nobody knows the cause of her illness. In her trembling and in her dying and in her mystery she clutches at an image on its way to disappearance. As the image fades, so will she.

The image I drew of the people by the freeway is also one of suspension in time and of disappearance. The woman—if she is a woman—is busy sewing the man into a bag, her hand poised over both him and herself as if she too will be enclosed, self-enclosed, and will eventually disappear. The two of them lie at the mouth of the tunnel, neither inside nor outside, just as they lie half in and half out of the bag that will, in all likelihood, be their shroud.

This threshold involves the same alternating current moving inside and outside as I have described for *yagé*-inspired healing images, and this is surely as intimately connected to the *seeing seeing* that Juan Bosco talked about, which, so it seems to me, is also a doubt, a doubting seeing, an hallucinogenic seeing, a seeing that doubts itself, so strange is the perception, a seeing that doubles itself such as my drawing of the people by the freeway.

If the art is right, then this sort of *seeing* stands a good chance of shaking off the sorcery that will otherwise take all from you and eventually finish you off. Perhaps the fear of that is even worse. Put otherwise, I am tempted to say that my drawing of the people by the tunnel is a visual equivalent of the healing I attempted in the sugarcane plantation town. And in this regard it seems to me relevant that six months before I drew my drawing of the people by the freeway tunnel, I was taking *yagé* with those dancing Kofan shamans shaking the bamboo floor, reactivating three decades of *yagé*-taking with Santiago Mutumbajoy. Thus in the notebook, after the words *I Swear I Saw This* had been written down, the drawing got drawn as if I needed not only to swear to the veracity—this *did* happen, this *is* truth—but needed to make an image so as to double the act of seeing with one's own eyes, because what I saw was more like an illusion. Doubting makes for doubling. Doubling the image through drawing, stroke by stroke, erasure by erasure, amounts to a laborious seeing. Eye and memory are painstakingly exercised or at least exercised in new ways. History is repeated in slow motion and the clumsiness of the artist actually adds to this *seeing seeing*, by which I mean to include as question the relationship between seeing and witnessing, which then transforms into something like Walter Benjamin's quickening heartbeat of the *jetztseit*—time of the standstill, time of the threshold—when an image surfaces at a moment of danger and just as quickly disappears if not seized. Like his Angel of History, which once upon a time was a little hunchback haunting the pages of a child's nursery rhyme book, our flatfooted fieldworking artist stares at the disaster growing ever higher as his taxi pulls him into the space of death, where little can be seen other than the movement of light and fumes.

11

For a long time after I was introduced to the world of *yagé* in 1972, I thought about something I got to call "the space of death." It helped me make sense of my *yagé* experience, blending personal worlds with a large historical view of the European conquest of the New World bringing into juxtaposition the spirit underworlds of Africa, Spain, and the Indians, with each group attributing power to the spirits of the Other, very much including the magic and sorcery entailed therein. This reflected my experience in the southwest of Colombia mixing with blacks, whites, and Indians, and listening to their stories about the powerful magic each other was supposed to possess.[1]

For me the space of death was a space of transgression, more like a time out of time in which anything could happen and catch you by surprise. As I figure it, this space of death allows for unworldly visitations and interior journeys, as by shamans with their hallucinogens, but it also occurs when terror strikes or the world falls apart, as with disease and tragedy and everyday states of emergency—such as being sewn into a nylon bag near the mouth of a freeway tunnel. Then, no shaman is necessary. The space is charged, "shamanic," one might say, all on its own. The deadest, which means the most alive, layers of this space of death are not innocent death but deaths due to what could be called the Conquest, the Ongoing Conquest, ongoing to the present day with the dislocation of people from the hinterlands by paramilitaries so as to make way first for cattle and bananas, and now cocaine plus African palm and sugarcane grown on lands often acquired through spectacular violence so as to provide biofuel for motor vehicles roaring into the mouth of the tunnel of what is blandly called "development," the last writing of the Great Experiment. At one point Benjamin referred to capitalism as a "phenomenon in which a new dream-filled sleep came over Europe, and, through it, a reactivation of mythic forces."[2] That certainly includes the space of death, the image of the people by the tunnel being exactly that—a reactivation of mythic force.

Some time has passed since I last drank *yagé*, but the kick it gives to the visual imagination lingers. I fall back on images of the late 1980s, high on the sandy banks of an oxbow lake looped out of the Putumayo River ten miles upstream from Puerto Asís. I see the house perched on stilts, open to the forest behind and the lake below, smooth pitch black. The night is pitch black too. A solitary light glows on an upturned canoe on which men sit, quietly smoking. Poverty lines the faces of the women, aged way beyond their years. There is despair in their eyes. But they joke and laugh. Even the woman in the bright red dress, La Pola,

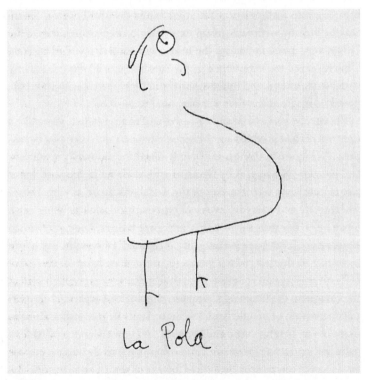

La Pola

with her grotesque abdominal swelling and her stick arms and legs, would smile. I drew her from memory days later in my notebook.

Yesterday—some twenty-five years after this night by the lake—I was shocked to come across the following photograph of La Pola in between two colonist women. Looking at it, I feel despair like a knife puncturing my soul. What I want to say is that this too is *yagé*, the wonderful world of wonders that is *yagé* that hipsters now swallow in Brooklyn and Amsterdam, and yes! it may be holy, and yes! it may be uplifting, but it is sad and desperate beyond words as well, this world of the poor colonist in which today *yagé* is sought out to perform its miracles.

Here the photograph speaks to me more than the drawing, perhaps because I had not seen it in twenty-five years and it brought the scene back in a rush. But the complementarity is noteworthy too, for the photograph is real in the ways photographs are, while the drawing is an accentuation of that reality. The drawing pulls out a feature—that grotesquely swollen stomach that rightfully would have the sick person in a hospital bed—and adds to it that vigilant, frightened eye suspended by those crazy stick feet like those of a bird. This is the person, or rather the *persona* that sticks in my mind, as much an archetype as the flesh-and-blood person rendered by the photograph.

Invited by these ailing colonist women, the shaman lay in a hammock. He was old and had come a long way by road and river and for-

Espantos coming up and down through the mist

est paths with me as his companion. We drank *yagé* and waited. Nausea acquired shapes. It grew cold.

The shaman chuckled, then started singing, curing a baby held in his lap in the darkness with its mother close by. There was a sigh. A body fell. We shrieked. La Pola had collapsed. She lay with only the whites of her eyes showing, to all appearances dead, a moaning tent-like mass feebly waving spidery arms and legs.

For hours she lay between life and death. Women wrapped in shawls went out of the hut down the ladder into the mist rising from the black lake, and then they would ascend back up again like the spirits of purgatory—*ánimas solas*—wandering, wailing ghosts.

The shaman's song wailed too, pulling us into the flesh-and-blood land of the living, away from the space of death into which the same song had tipped us. But we were on an insane roll, lost in the darkness of the lake and the rising mist through which these hooded women emerged and descended. At every step La Pola's moans threatened to outdo the song. Only our faces emerged from the mist—those same faces I saw in my mind years later while attempting to cure a young woman in a plantation town—faces leaning forward, faces catching the light, faces of people far more at home with spirits than I was, and that was good enough for me to keep going with my wordless song that would later become my wordless drawing of the people by the freeway.

12

Walter Benjamin was interested in hallucinatory experience too. In fact much of his writing has a hallucinatory tug to it, for example in his fastidious eye for details, in each one of which, as with William Blake's grain of sand, lies a universe. This mode of perception is enlarged upon in his hashish trances, in which he speaks fulsomely of reality as "ornament" involving the consciousness of having suddenly penetrated "that most hidden, generally most inaccessible world of surfaces," such as occurs in childhood or with a fever.[1] Characterized by multivalence and plurality of configuration, Benjamin assured his "shaman," Dr. Frankel, that "Ornaments are colonies of spirits."[2] Yet it was most especially language that Benjamin kept hallucinating about. Taking hashish, words kept piling themselves into his visions, playing with each other, severing syllables in orgies of autodeconstruction, sending out wildly unexpected but beautiful associations. Words, or rather wordplay, were his pictures. These he called *constellations*, a tribute to his abiding passion for astrology and for what he called "the doctrine of the similar."

In his memoir, "Berlin Childhood around 1900," Benjamin recalls how, as a kid, he would sometimes unintentionally distort words without intending to—a common enough childhood experience, and one that Michel Leiris makes much of in his essay "The Sacred in Everyday Life." But Benjamin extends and explores such distortion in remarkable directions. "If in this way I distorted both myself and the world," he writes, "I did only what I had to do to gain a foothold in life. Early on, I learned to disguise myself in words, which really were clouds. The gift of perceiving similarities is, in fact, nothing but a weak remnant of the old compulsion to become similar and to behave mimetically. In me, however, this compulsion acted through words."[3]

"I'd like to write something," he said while taking hashish in 1931, "that comes from things the way wine comes from grapes."[4] From this it was but a short step to the most audacious mimetic power of all, the magic tricks Benjamin dubbed *dialectical images*, images that incubate history in their midst, containing a *before* and a *now* that, when combined, can make for "a Messianic cessation of happening, or, put differently, a revolutionary chance in the fight for the oppressed past."[5]

What characterizes the dialectical image is its sudden appearance and equally sudden disappearance, hence the need to grasp it before it disappears if we are to get close to the utopian promise of the Messianic return. Could it be that neither we nor the image on its own are quite up to the task? Could it be that what is required is ritual in which, as with *yagé*, bodies, both human and nonhuman, are activated?

There seems to me no doubt that Benjamin's idea of the dialectical image was an idea that understood pictures as blended with the human body as well as with language. Here we verge on the incantatory language of *I Swear I Saw This*, where language enters the body of the world. The "long-sought image sphere" he claims in his essay on surrealism, is "the best room" in the world of "universal and integral actualities." It is the sphere, "in a word, in which political materialism and physical nature share the inner man . . . the sphere of images and, more concretely, of bodies."[6] And what makes for revolution—remember, this is 1928 Western Europe—what will fulfill the transcendence of reality prescribed by *The Communist Manifesto*, as he puts it, is the *interpenetration of body with image.*

Is this why I am so fond of the image of him lying catatonic on the floor? Here he lies stiller than still, our great champion of the body—under the influence of hashish, closely observed by his cousin Egon Wissing, who is taking notes. Benjamin is talking about toys and colored pictures meant for children. He sees a field roller with its handle hidden deeply in grain. Pulled by goblins, this field roller is ripening the seed. He has his left arm raised in the air with the index finger poking up, *for at least an hour*. An hour! The hand masks itself, he explains. It is covered with glazed paper in different colors. The arm is a lookout tower, or rather an "insight tower." Images go in and they go out.[7]

Like Bosco, Benjamin not only acted out his hallucinated images but made drawings of them. And what strange drawings they are! There were words in cursive script forming alliterative sentences such as "Sheep my little sleep sheep" repeated several times with slight variations so as to form a shape like a halo or an ear. There were words forming a title, "Veritable sorceresses," repeated four times with differing accentuation of the letters. And there are two rough sketches that could be called figurative. One is called "Protected/forbidden bird," the other, "Frog making a survey." (The frog brings to mind Benjamin's fist and index finger emitting images from the "insight tower.")

What the words indicate to me is what Benjamin referred to as *nonsensuous correspondences.* Think back to his wish "I'd like to write something that comes from things the way wine comes from grapes" as an example of such a correspondence. After all, as a child in Berlin he had had to distort both himself and the world to gain a foothold in life and did so by disguising himself in words, which were really clouds. Later in life there was hashish, which accelerated the compulsion to *perceive* similarities, and that to the extent of *becoming* similar, in this case through the medium of written words.[8] Hence what we see in Benjamin's hallucinatory drawings is the transition from grapes to wine in graceful arabesques.

If we proceed further along this chain from words to images, we are in for a surprise because what mediates this transition are spirits. The first words Benjamin (our great materialist) ever wrote down about his hashish experiences are: "Spirits hover (vignette style) over my right shoulder. Coldness in that shoulder." While a page later he notes: "Afterward, in the café with Hessel, a brief farewell to the spirit world."[9]

The images come and go with terrific speed—similar in their dazzling ephemerality to the coming and going of images he later wrote about in 1940 in his desperate "Theses on the Philosophy of History."

Frog making a survey

These theses on the occult meaning of history were his last writing, claiming the spirit power upon which Marxism, unbeknownst to itself, depended.

Repeatedly in the theses Benjamin alluded to the coming of the Messiah in the struggle against fascism, while Bosco and his father speak of undoing sorcery, also by means of an image that flashes forth at a moment of danger. "Each to his own," you mutter. Yet surely Benjamin's version is intellectually and, for that matter, morally superior, because he brings the theory of *history* (that great God word) to the perceptions of hashish intoxication. But does not sorcery go straight to the marrow?

Like fieldwork, to imbibe hashish means to travel to parts unknown accompanied more often than not by a feeling of anguish that one cannot communicate the experience without compromising it. Let us recall the mute "insight tower" emitting and receiving images, the body stretched out on the floor, left arm held high with its index finger pointing for an hour. What on earth is this finger pointing to?

This is where the fieldwork diary no less than Benjamin's drawings and bodily gestures come into their own because of the way they hold the communicable in fruitful tension with the incommunicable. As I have been at pains to point out earlier, the fieldwork diary is built upon a sense of failure—a foreboding sense that the writing is always inadequate to the experience it records. Nevertheless, on rereading by its author, the diary has the potential to bring forth a shadow text that can simulate the experience that gave birth to the diary entry, not only for what is said, but more likely for what is omitted yet exists in gestures between the words. This Barthes called the "role of the Phantom, of the Shadow."[10] In other words, the diary is likely to contain these distinct modes of experience that we can call "explicit" and "implicit." The explicit is the more tedious, hardworking attempt to dutifully copy what went on. It belongs to *homo faber*, the world of work. Barthes hates this property of the diary.

But the implicit mode? That is another story altogether. It is geared toward atmosphere and imagery, where and when spaces between words are mined by gesture. This belongs to *homo ludens*, the world of play, and it is toward this world, thanks to hashish, that the catatonic man lying on his back point us.

Here I think of two friends of mine in the Putumayo River basin in southwest Colombia, the Indian shaman I have referred to, and his old friend Florencio, an Ingano- and Spanish-speaking Indian who, like the shaman, was an avid taker of *yagé*. While the shaman rarely spoke, if at all, of his *yagé* experiences, Florencio, who always wanted to become a healer but never did, spoke a great deal and beautifully about his. It was as if between them there existed this division of mystical or at least poetic labor: the person who could see but not speak required the person who could speak but not see, and by "see," I mean that special vision that allows the shaman to mystically pass on his vision to the sick person without having to say anything.

It was Florencio who told me of his experience accompanying a healer who was trying to cure a woman sick with headaches. They drank *yagé*. First he saw angels coming from the sky with lightning-bolt crystals in their hands to press on his tongue—so he would speak well—and into his chest—so he would be of pure heart—and then how the angels in a flash changed into wild birds strutting around and eventually filling the room—"pure birds," the room was the essence of birds—and then the birds in a flash changed into *another painting*—as he put it, *otra pinta*—this time of soldiers of the Colombian army dressed in gold and dancing like Indian shamans, who themselves are said to dance like the spirits of *yagé*.

These images, Florencio says, were wordlessly passed on to him by the healer in the altered mental state—the *chuma*—of *yagé*. Florencio struggled to climb out of his hammock and join in dancing with the soldiers. But he was unable. "Seeing that, you cure?" he asked the shaman, who replied, "Yes *amigo*, seeing that, you cure."

This division of hallucinogenic labor between the vocally expressible and inexpressible, between the patient and the healer, between the one who speaks but cannot "see," and the one who "sees" but cannot, or will not, speak, parallels what goes on with the fieldworker's diary. To whom does one write when one writes a diary? That is the question motivating me throughout this inquiry. What does it mean to say *I Swear I Saw This*? Florencio stands to the image-generating shaman as the fieldworker's diary does to the fieldworker's experience. It is Florencio, who cannot see, who gives voice to the mute envisioning of the shaman. This provides a model of text-image interchange suggesting why I feel the need to draw in my notebook, mysteriously reenacting that healer-patient visual interchange. What my drawing of the people by the tunnel brings out, I feel, is one of the more acute moments when this twofold, generative character of complementary opposites expresses itself *as an act bearing witness*.

Struggling to get out of his hammock to dance with the dancing soldiers dressed in gold, the guy who cannot see suddenly gets it.

"Seeing that, you cure?" he asks.

Here witnessing is well nigh miraculous. The emblematic power of the nation-state with its soldiers wrought in gold provides the image that you can build into your own, dancing self, enhancing the sense of the marvelous.

But as for the vision of the people by the tunnel, what we see is the opposite of the dancing soldiers aglow with golden fire dancing like shamans, themselves dancing like the spirits of *yagé*. Here all is stock-still and entombed as if the very restlessness of the souls of those who have died a violent death throughout Colombia needs to be triply contained, first by the shroud of the nylon bag, second by the concrete walls of the freeway, and third by the tunnel itself, into which roar the dancing automobiles aglow with fire.

13

Anthropologists aren't the only ones with fieldwork notebooks. One noted intellectual, Walter Benjamin, seems to have been lost without one. "At any rate," writes Hannah Arendt, "nothing was more characteristic of him in the thirties than the very little notebooks with black covers which he always carried with him and in which he tirelessly entered in the form of quotations what daily living and reading netted him in the way of 'pearls' and 'coral.'"[1] The reference is to Shakespeare's *Tempest*.

> *Full fathom five thy father lies,*
> *Of his bones are coral made,*
> *Those are pearls that were his eyes.*
> *Nothing of him that doth fade*
> *But doth suffer a sea-change*
> *Into something rich and strange.*

The allusion to pearls and coral suggests that a notebook is likely to transform the everyday into an opalescent underwater world where laws of motion are suspended. Like moonwalkers, the writer in a notebook can take giant steps freed from the pull of gravity as reality is rendered in baroque forms like pearls and coral. As for quotations, they are especially empowered so as to disrupt context and create new worlds, as does a fieldworker's notebook "quoting" from everyday experience. The unconscious of the world, so to speak, meets up with the unconscious of the mind. Arendt emphasizes the surreal impact of the entries. Next to a poem such as "The First Snow" was a report from Vienna dated summer 1939 saying that the local gas company "had stopped supplying gas to Jews. The gas consumption of the Jewish population involved a loss for the gas company, since the biggest consumers were the one who did not pay their bills. The Jews used the gas especially for committing suicide."[2]

Benjamin had long wanted to publish a collection of his quotations. This came to pass long after his death with the publication of *The Arcades Project*, a hefty tome of 954 pages in the English translation. He referred to the only book (other than his dissertation) he published in his lifetime, *One Way Street*, not as a book but as a notebook.[3] It consisted of surreal, aphoristic observations.

In this regard his views on *collecting* are every bit as important as his valuation of *the quotation*. He characterized a "genuine" collection as a *magic encyclopedia* on account of what he saw as its occult properties and its divinatory propensities.[4] We might think here of any collection whatsoever, but the collection that makes up a notebook, whether of quotations or snatches of everyday experience, would seem especially appropriate to what he had in mind. The idea is this: because chance plays a part in how the items in a collection gravitate into one's hands, a collection can be used as an instrument of divination, since chance is the flipside of fate.

For sure this is a wild idea, like what you find with private investigator Clem Snide in trying to solve the case of a missing man— presumed dead—by listening at random to sound recordings he has made in the missing man's empty villa in Greece a hundred feet from the beach. The investigator's recorder is "specially designed for cutins and overlays and you can switch from Record to Playback without stopping the machine."[5] He records the toilet flushing and the shower running, the blinds being raised, the rattle of dishes, and the sound of the sea and wind as he walks along the beach. He records as well the disco music to which the missing man danced. He cuts in by reading sections from *The Magus* as well as by "thinking out loud" about the case. Later he randomly chooses different sections of the recordings. At the same time he watches TV to ensure that he listens only subconsciously to what he has recorded. "I've cracked cases like this with nothing to go on, just by getting out and walking around at random," he says.[6]

Here chance determines—what an odd phrase!—what goes into

the collection, and chance determines how it is to be magically used as an artful series of sound cut-ups, such as Brion Gysin and Ian Sommerville played with in the early sixties. But I wish to appropriate yet another feature from the magic of the *magic encyclopedia* and this is the way the notebook is actually an extension of oneself if not more self than oneself, like an entirely new organ alongside one's heart and brain, to name but the more evocative organs of our inner self. What this new organ does is incorporate other worlds into one's own. Is this not obvious when Benjamin himself states that the genuine collector's objects do not come alive in him, but rather it is he who lives in them?[7]

This I will call a *fetish*—an object we hold so dear as to seem possessed by spiritual power. While it is a *thing*—with all the inertness we may attach to a material object—it is nevertheless revered to the extent that it can come to stand over you and turn you into its willing accomplice, if not your slave. What is meant to be a mere instrument or a tool, a mere notebook, ends up being a whole lot more.

This was the gist of what Marx sardonically suggested in *Capital* when he coined the notion of *commodity fetishism*, meaning that today we live in a world wherein the products of our labor and especially money become endowed with life to the extent they escape our control and come to dominate us, often with devastating results, for example, the current financial meltdown of the world. So it was with God, the product of man's imagination, who turned the tables and told man that he, the one and only God, had created man. But with your hardworking 24/7 fetish, like a magical charm, the situation is not quite so one-sided. The fetish has to come through. It is revered, of course, but it is also commanded and expected to perform magical work.

What irony that the anthropologist, namely myself, given to studying fetishism, should have unwittingly developed with his notebooks a fetish all of his own and become not only a slave to his fetish but enamored of it—to the degree that here I am writing an entire book about notebooks![8] There were those occasional cane cutters where I was living who, paid by the ton cut, were rumored to be in league with the devil. Hiding a wooden figurine in the undergrowth, they would cut a swath through the cane toward it while uttering strange cries so as to magically harvest well above the average worker. And there was me, the anthropologist, recording all this in my notebook full of its own strange cries.

The cane cutters might have their mysterious figurines, but I had my mysterious notebooks, which sure improved productivity, comparable to tons cut, and the notebooks did this because they were not a dumping ground or parking lot for information. They swiftly became "ends in themselves" and thus actively encouraged contributions from the field, the field being of course both observer and observed and the observer observed. The notebooks became hungry for input, like the demons I have read about in the stomachs of witches in Cameroon, demons that were initially allies in self-advancement, but ever-ready to turn on their masters.[9]

But Benjamin's fetishes are more endearing. "I carry the blue book with me everywhere," he wrote in a letter of thanks to Alfred Cohn in 1927, "and speak of nothing else. And I am not the only one—other people too beam with pleasure when they see it. I have discovered that it has the same colors as a certain pretty Chinese porcelain: its blue glaze is in the leather, its white in the paper and its green in the stitching. Others compare it to shoes from Turkistan. I am sure there is nothing else of this kind as pretty in the whole of Paris, despite the fact that, for all its timelessness and unlocatedness, it is also quite modern and Parisian."[10]

Could this be a case of what Sir James George Frazer of *The Golden Bough* called "homeopathic" magic, the magic of *like affecting like*? For does not Benjamin use the fetish of the notebook in order to ride on the back of the fetishism that has, according to his interpretation of Marxism, come to define the modern world? In other words, his strategy of alliance with the fetishism of commodities as a framework of thought and analysis involves first and foremost his instrument of research—his notebook—as fetish.

What is more, the fetish character of the notebook with its "pearls" and "coral" is here fated into existence by its being from the beginning more than an object. It is a gift. Hence it carries something of "the spirit of the gift," something alive, obligating the recipient to reciprocate, and this Benjamin does fulsomely in his thank-you letter to Cohn, providing something charming in return—charm for charm—giving over something wonderful of himself that the gift of the notebook draws out.

What goes into this gift that is Benjamin's notebook? What exactly are its "pearls" and "coral"? Surely they are the spawn of the world historical joust between gift and commodity, and in this manner they parallel the actions of those characters close to Benjamin's heart; namely the *gambler*, the *flaneur*, and, of course, the *collector*. For these are the characters who stand on the threshold of the market with one foot inside, the other outside, and they stalk through each and every of the 954 pages of *The Arcades Project.*

Apart from Alfred Cohn's gift, there are other notebooks of Benjamin that have been saved, and they too suggest that their owner cathected onto them because of their material detail, as when he confesses to what he calls his "shameful weakness" for the "extremely thin, transparent, yet excellent stationery, which I am unfortunately unable to find anyplace around here."[11]

Fastidious. Obsessive. And something more. This "something more" is not lost on the editors and collectors of Benjamin's remains, as when they write in *Walter Benjamin's Archive*—a book as handsome and as finely crafted as what it sets out to describe—of the "almost magical quality" and of what they call the "cult" value that the notebooks possessed for their owner. Indeed they seem to have caught quite a dose of the fetish bug themselves, as when they tell us that the "chamois-colored paper of a notebook bound in cardboard, with notes, drafts of critiques and diary entries from the years 1929–1934, is thicker and has–crosswise and longwise—a fine line structure."[12]

Big deal! you say. Well, yes! It is a big deal, being thicker and finer like that. The devil is in the details.

Yet that degree of absorption into the thingness of the thing is nothing compared with the illustrations the editors provide of some of the notebooks—for example, the full-page color photograph of what they entitle *Notebook Ms. Leather cover (1927/1929).* Here the entire page is nothing more—or should I say "nothing more," given the strange laws of the fetish—"nothing more" than a black rectangle with a slightly uneven top edge and traces of unevenness in the surface.[13] It is a color plate but the object has no color, the nothingness of which gleams with occult significance. "You can take our picture," winks the fetish, "but you can't take our power."

This fetishization of the fetish makes me want to ask whether we should not check our enthusiasm for the doodles and scribbles of Great Men. Why are we immediately attracted to this time-out side of greatness?

Take Le Corbusier's seventy-three notebooks—I mean sketchbooks. Yes! Seventy- three, and all, as far as I know, published in over four thousand pages containing a photographic replica of each of the original pages. What he wanted were editions that would reach the widest possible audience, to scatter his seed among the masses. "Corbu" is how our architecture librarian refers to him, like a pet dog or pop idol. His books occupy a special niche behind the reserve desk. I open the page of volume 1, published by MIT Press. I can barely handle the weight of the book with just one hand. Volume 1 covers the years 1914–48. By way of a table of contents, there are rows of undistinguished tiny grey rectangles, which, on closer inspection, turn out to be photographs of the covers of thirteen sketchbooks, one after the other, that make up this time period. Such reverence! Like the crown jewels. Some have an obscure doodling on them, others a date, like "Paris/1918." When you turn to the sketches themselves, the gap between the esteem aroused by the object and its pictorial representation as an object is woefully large—which raises the question, *Why bother?* What is the need here— the need to grasp the object as an image up close?

With this question we hit upon a profound and disturbing truth regarding notebooks: that they may be fetishized by their *owners*, but how much more so by their *followers*, like the editors of Benjamin's and of Corbu's notebooks. It seems as if notebooks are thought to provide the inside track to the soul of the person writing or drawing in them. It is like being privy to the secrets of an alchemist's laboratory, enlivened by their all too human foibles.

And are we not all of us followers? Is not this conceit about the inside track something we cleave to and what, in fact, lies behind my own interest in the value of notebooks? We think we are watching a mind at work and can, as it were, eavesdrop. But really, when we open up to almost any page of Corbu's sketchbooks, we don't know what to think. It is all frightfully obscure, like a genius doodling to his muse. We are left at best with the warm glow of having warmed our souls at the fire of creation.

"When travelling with Le Corbusier," writes the author of the preface, "one often saw him take a notebook from his pocket in order to record something he had just thought of or seen. At these moments Le Corbusier drew as one would take notes, without trying to make a pretty picture simply to imprint upon his memory some central idea, to remember, and assimilate it. He often said, 'Don't take photographs, draw; photography interferes with seeing, drawing etches in the mind.' He would jot down those spontaneous phrases that cannot be repeated, too vague for anything but one's notebook."[14]

The notebook is enchanted as well as enchanting, at least from afar. The way it slips in and out of the Great Man's pocket. It is all body, too. Forget photography. It gets between subject and object. Go corporeal. Draw! A photograph captures only the surface, but the notebook gets at the deep truth of things. Full grammatical sentences? Forget it. Just jot. And jot some more. Short-circuit language and me, the writer, too. Such is the idea of the notebook at its mystical best. Fetish of the fetish. Inside of the inside.

14

There is a disquieting rhythm to my own notebooks. I keep them only when travelling, when engaged in what I think of as fieldwork. I do not and cannot keep a diary, journal, notebook—call it what you will—when at home, what I will call "home," although that is a long way across a huge ocean of sea and memory.

The editors of *Walter Benjamin's Archive* (a book about Benjamin's notebooks) note that Benjamin was frequently travelling and that he loved to write while on the move *wherever he happened to find himself.* This parallels an anthropologist's notebook. "Could he have found a more faithful companion for all that than his notebooks?" they ask.[1] And I in turn must ask what could more faithfully express the fetish quality of the notebook than its being described as a "faithful companion," yet how sad, too, given the loneliness of its owner. Are we to assume that the notebook is an alter ego, that it is this strange entity to whom you write in your notebook, making of it—this mere object of paper (and its smart leather cover)—a keenly receptive human being, thirsty for more?

In fact as early as 1913, aged twenty-one, Benjamin habitually kept a diary when travelling, noting, that "the diary questions existence and 'gives depth to time.'"[2] Such a statement seems to me to go a good deal further philosophically than most anthropological fieldwork notebooks, but the potential is always there just under the surface, even though the absence of such insight is rather shocking. For of all people, should it not be the ever vigilant, culturally and self-aware anthropologist, who should be sensitive to how travel questions existence and gives depth to time?

Le Corbusier's seventy-three sketchbooks are nearly all travelogues, all four-thousand-plus pages: South America, Moscow, the Spanish border, Spain, Barcelona, Majorca, Algeria, Monte Carlo, Madrid, Rio, a Liberty ship named the *Vernon S. Hood*; Bogotá, Barranquilla, Marseille, New York, Ahmendabad (India), India, Milan, Chandigarh, Ronchamp, Bombay, Tokyo, Kyoto, Rome, Zurich, Stockholm, Cambridge, Boston, Turin, Strasburg, Brasilia, etc. These are the titles on the covers of separate sketchbooks, and I have not included the repeat visits, of which there are many.

Burroughs had his travel notebook too. He would, he says, divide the page into three columns. The first would have the more or less factual elements of the journey—checking in at the airport departure desk, what the clerks are saying, other things he overhears, and so forth. The second contained what these things made him remember. And the third, what he called his "reading column," consisted of quotations from books he had taken with him that connect with his journey. He found the connections extraordinary, "if you really keep your eyes open."[3]

The notebook is like a magical object in a fairytale. It is a lot more than an object, as it inhabits and fills out hallowed ground between meditation and production. Truly, writing is a strange business. "He was fueled by ambition to fill them," comment the editors of *Walter Benjamin's Archive*.[4] Without the notebook, *nada!* Or at least very little, although I note mythical exceptions, such as Edmund Leach, who wrote his classic *Political Systems of Highland Burma* after losing most of his fieldwork notebooks when he fled the Japanese army in Burma during WWII.[5]

This story is lovingly told and retold to the extent that you can't help but wonder if many of us would actually like to free ourselves of our notes and write fresh like a bird on the wing. But that seems sacrilege. Only if the Japanese army is on your tail—or else if you're the victim of arson—can you do that, as we shall soon see.

Was this loss connected to—or fated by—Leach's feisty attempt to later overthrow the stable equilibrium model of society that dominated British social anthropology? In a way he overthrew nothing. What he did was reestablish that model of social equilibrium on a higher plane, preserving the cycle of social transformation from anarchy to hierarchy and back again over a longer time period. This cycle parallels the cycle of loss and rediscovery.

Yet the story of loss is not clear cut. First of all, the man actually did write notes (lots and lots, I presume). So one very important function in keeping a notebook was fulfilled because simply going through the exercise of writing down observations and thoughts therein is so helpful to one's sense of being and intellectual machinations such that loss is not necessarily all that much of a loss. It is not all that important what goes into the notebook, compared with the mere fact of having the notebook in hand and spending time each day writing. Second, not all the notes were lost. They had a scattered history and existed in different places and some could be retrieved—testimony to the fact that the mere concept of "the fieldnotes" as something unitary and monadic (and without copies) is woefully simpleminded and wonderfully fetishistic.

We see this too with another mythical and equally dramatic case of loss, not because of the Japanese army but because of fire—arson at the height of protests on U.S. campuses during the Vietnam War— in the sacred precincts of the Center for Advanced Studies in the Behavioral Sciences at Stanford devouring all three copies of M. N. Srinivas's fieldnotes of his village study carried out in 1948 in Mysore, India, twenty-two years earlier. (Why did he have three copies anyway, one might reasonably ask?) Srinivas went on to write by memory an outstanding ethnography, *The Remembered Village*, even though the loss of the notes was speedily recovered by having a copy (again!) of his original notes in Delhi flown over and also because of the patient labor of a group of faculty wives raking through the debris and piecing a copy of sorts together. Such dedication! Not only anthropologists think of their notes like the crown jewels! But in the meantime Srinivas had decided to go it alone and write from memory anyway, with the unexpected and delightful consequence—so unlike the case of Leach—that the book became very author-centered, as that's how he allowed his remembering to gather force and momentum.

In other words, the drama of loss—like losing one's child or lover— provides testimony to the mighty power of the notebook, whose loss can actually provide more of a notebook effect than the notebook itself. The loss of a notebook—and who has not suffered this terrible fate at least once in their lifetime?—opens out onto the great emptiness from which the subsequently published monograph draws its strength. Behind the lost notebook stands the ghost notebook. (What does the fetishist do when he loses his fetish?)

The converse is no less true. How many notebook keepers go on to complete their projects without once consulting their notebook? A lot, that's for sure. So long as the notebook is there in its thereness you don't have to open the cover. There is something absurdly comforting in the existence of the trinity consisting of:

- you
- the event
- and the event notated as a notebook entry

For now you can, as it were, proceed to walk upright and maybe even on water without having to consult the entry. Simply knowing it is there provides the armature of truth, of the "this happened," that, like a rock climber's crampons, allows you to scale great heights.

This is why the materiality of the notebook attracts so much attention. Because it is a contraption—a marvelous contraption—that stands in for thought, experience, history, and writing. The materiality of the notebook received from Alfred Cohn is adorable. It is beautiful, as the blue of Chinese porcelain. How wonderfully polished, fragile, far away, and exotic is the indefinable quality of texture and light that is the "glaze" of blueness in the leather! And then there is the whiteness of the paper and the green of the stitching that holds the whole thing together.

The green stitching. Could Benjamin be green-stitching himself into his notebook as he speaks of it, like the homeless woman (if she is a woman) sewing the man into the bag at the entrance to the tunnel of the freeway? Is a notebook a way of squirreling yourself away from the world and stealing its secrets to line your burrow?

At one point Benjamin appeals to his notebook benefactor, Alfred Cohn, for another notebook because "I cannot contemplate the prospect of soon having to write homeless thoughts again."[6] But it is he who is homeless.

To the materiality of the notebook we should add the materiality of

Simryn Gill's "Pearls"

the language as manifest by the microscopic writing of the notebook. Benjamin could pack an entire essay onto one page. In the sixty-three pages of one notebook, for instance, there are the drafts of complete transcriptions of over twenty essays. "The writing of a man in prison," Klaus Neumann once told me. Then there is the care Benjamin took with graphic form in his notebooks. There are, it seems, plenty of Dada-like layouts and lush color such that the subheadings in green, yellow, blue, red, and orange leap out at you.

Simryn Gill has taken this mix of materiality and poetry a step further, as with the pearl necklace she sent me from Australia, each pearl being made of a line or two cut out from essays written by Benjamin.[7] Which essays did she choose? Benjamin's essays on collecting, "Unpacking My Library," a letter to Gershom Scholem, and "Berlin

Childhood." Fifty years after Hannah Arendt's pearl diver, this ultimate transformation—this ultimate materialization—takes us back to the "sea change into something rich and strange," which I wear as thankfully as Benjamin received his blue-glazed notebook with green stitching from Alfred Cohn in 1927.

15

So much for the *notebook*. But here I must pause to address the difference between the *notebook*, that provisionary receptacle of inspired randomness, and the *diary*, that more or less steady confidante of the daily round.

At the outset I am struck by the polarized reactions I have come across with respect to keeping a diary. While I find the diary form congenial to my work, others are disdainful. I have met anthropologists who tell me they can't bear to look at their field diary because it is so boring. Roland Barthes is so disdainful that he refers to the "diary disease." Even so, the polarized reaction exists within Barthes as well, and momentously so—as with the *Mourning Diary* he kept for two years, starting the day after his mother died.[1]

Before *that* diary he detected a strange mechanism at work in what he calls "the interstices of notation," such that a typically mundane diary entry (waiting for a bus at seven in the evening under a cold rain in the rue de Rivoli in Paris) makes him recall—on rereading—the grayness of the atmosphere *precisely because it is not recorded*. But it is no use, he claims, to describe that atmosphere now, as "I would lose it again instead of some other silenced sensation, and so on . . . role of the Phantom, of the Shadow."[2]

I take this intriguing observation to be a striking endorsement of Freud's idea of the mystic writing pad, that the moment an observation is processed—in this case by writing, as on the mystic writing pad or in the diary—it disappears. But in disappearing, and unlike what Freud says, it creates a "nest" or a shadow, what Barthes calls "the Phantom." Of course, with respect to the diary, the stuff written down does not literally disappear. It is there and remains there on the page, even if it is never looked at again by my anthropologist friend who finds her diary boring. But if she ventures forth to turn the pages it is likely that some *silenced sensation* emerges upon rereading. Truly writing is a complicated business—this is what diary writing reveals—but not nearly as complex as reading, especially rereading what one has written about one's recent past.

I think of Barthes's *Phantom* as belonging to the same family of representational familiars as does the *third meaning*, which he discerns in the film image or the *punctum* he writes about later in *Camera Lucida*. It is what Joan Didion directs our attention toward in her essay "On Keeping a Notebook," but unlike Barthes she finds it useful, indeed inspiring, to tug at the Phantom.

She too has little time for diaries. Like Barthes she has tried to keep a diary, but whenever she tries dutifully to record the day's events she is overcome, she says, by boredom.[3] The results, she says, "are mysterious at best." And why mysterious? "What is this business," she writes, "about 'shopping, typing piece, dinner with E, depressed'? Shopping for what? Typing what piece?" And so on.

But a notebook—her notebook—is different from a diary. For Didion, notebooks have nothing to do with the factual record of the daily round. They contain what I would call "sparks," or, better yet, dry tinder, which in the right hands at the right moment will burst into flame. Perhaps I should call this dry tinder "interstices of notation." In other words, the notebook lies at the outer reaches of language and order. It lies at the outer reaches of language because it represents the chance pole of a collection, rather than the design pole. It is more open to chance than the diary, for example, which is ordered by the arrow of time. In other words, the notebook page is all interstices— and, dare I say it, all Phantoms—impossible, but true. Impossible because interstices are spaces between things. But here there are no things. It's like having an unconscious without a conscious. Which takes us back to rereading one's diary, evoking the *silenced sensation*.

Yeats expresses pretty much the same idea when he jots the following down in his journal in 1909: "To keep these notes natural and useful to me I must keep one note from leading to another, that I may not surrender myself to literature. Every note must come as a casual thought, then it will be my life. Neither Christ nor Buddha nor

Socrates wrote a book, for to do that is to exchange life for a logical process."[4]

Offhandedly Didion wonders if the notes in her notebook would best be called *lies*, the sort of momentary observations a writer (of fiction?) might one day find useful, such as the entry: "That woman Estelle is partly the reason why George Sharp and I are separated today. *Dirty crepe-de Chine wrapper, hotel bar, Wilmington RR, 9:45 a.m. August Monday morning.*"

In fact, she starts her essay "On Keeping a Notebook" in media res with "That woman Estelle," thus triggering Barthes's mechanism of the Phantom. She has pulled at that thread and created a marvelous concoction, or should I say *concatenation* of events and ideas. "How much of it actually happened?" she asks at the end, when she has time to draw breath.[5]

She writes of the "girl from the Eastern Shore" leaving the man beside her, going back to the city, and all "she can see ahead are the viscous city sidewalks." The woman is worried about the hem of the plaid silk dress and wishes she could stay in that nice cool bar. . . .

In other words, the stray remark in the bar turns out to be the caption to a picture, to a string of pictures, and there are plenty of other "random" notes in her notebook that no doubt could be pulled at so as to release the Phantom therein. A line by Jimmy Hoffa: "I may have my faults but lying ain't one of them." A man checking his coat says to his friend, "That's my old football number." During 1964, 720 tons of soot fell on every square mile of New York City. This one is labeled "FACT."[6] Again recall surrealism's "found objects."

And so on. The notes in the notebook work the same as the visual "moments" that Barthes relishes in film as the "third meaning." Apart from what he called the information in any given image, and apart from its symbolic values, something else lurked in the background. "I receive (and probably even first and foremost) a third meaning," he wrote, "evident, erratic, obstinate," and he speaks of being "held" by the image.[7]

Yet for all the randomness—or apparent randomness—of the notes jotted down in her notebook, Didion sees a common thread. All these fragments of perception that lend themselves to pictures release something because they strike a chord and that chord is the author's life, which, like ours, keeps changing. The notebook—which, in her estimation, is strenuously opposed to the diary—is thus nevertheless a personal archive and something more: a collection that keeps the current self in touch with former selves through the medium of external observations and overheard remarks. (This sounds very like an anthropologist, I must say.) "It is a good idea," she notes, "to keep in touch, and I suppose that keeping in touch is what notebooks are all about."[8]

Writer as anthropologist? What was her notebook like when she was in El Salvador preparing her book on the Great Communicator's dirty little war there?[9] Big Brave America with Ronald Reagan leading the charge. How many nuns raped and killed by the United States supported troops and right-wing death squads? Archbishops assassinated?

But this is my real question: what about a diary of the daily round in that place at that time? No! Not much shopping there, I shouldn't think. Indeed, in an Other place the distinction between the *diary* and what she thinks of as a *notebook* tends to break down, I would think. "Role of the Phantom, of the Shadow."

This Other place can be right here, if you want to be literal about it, as with Didion's *The Year of Magical Thinking* about her husband's sudden death between Christmas and New Year of 2004 in their apartment in New York City at the time their only child was in a coma, which eventuated in death too.[10] What I am getting at is that Didion here (as elsewhere in her work) draws on many types of records and memories that have the feel of a diary. She draws on diarylike incidents, and in *The Year of Magical Thinking* she produces a text that is like an elaborated diary written in the present tense or having the intense feel of a diary recording the present in scenes and flashbacks in cliffhanging detail.

The point is that a fieldworker's diary is about experience in a field of strangeness. It is not about waiting for the bus to take you to your accustomed, safe abode so that you can write another article on the death of the author. A fieldworker's diary retains loyalty to Didion's "touching." It retains loyalty to feelings and experience within the field that is fieldwork, such that it merges with the aforementioned notebook where the Phantom who inhabits the interstices of notation roams.

Writer as anthropologist? W. G. Sebald invokes the notebook in his meditation on the absurdly difficult task of writing about the terrible violence inflicted on the civilian population of Germany by the Allies during WWII. The problem is first that of representing violence, and second that the huge numbers of victims are generally seen as deserving their fate ,which has to include becoming invisible to history. Sebald cites as helpmate Alexander Kluge's "archaeological excavations of the slag heaps of our collective existence" and notes how Kluge's *Neue Geschicten* (*New Stories*) resists traditional literary forms "by presenting the preliminary collection and organization of textual and pictorial material, both historical and fictional, straight from the author's notebooks."[11] Sebald emphasizes the merit of disorder in such a mode of presentation ("across a wide field of reality"), together with the subjective involvement and commitment.

Writer as anthropologist? "Put all the images in language in a place of safety," writes Jean Genet in his last book, *Prisoner of Love*, "and make use of them, for they are in the desert, and it's in the desert we must go and look for them." He certainly did. Like an anthropologist, only more audacious, more self-involved, and with no research grant, several times he thus ventured—creating ethnographic, diary-based, crossover literature, neither fish nor fowl where the unwritten thrives because of the written, midway between fiction and nonfiction, coming from the hand of the thief, sexual nonconformist, convict, and camp follower of the PLF.

Writer as anthropologist as imagist? This is the *place of safety* to which Genet refers us, and it is like Didion's notebook or an anthropologist's diary. There they hibernate, those "images in language," like spirits of the dead. Do not all writers have their familiars? As in Barthes's "interstices of notation," the images have to be exiled, as it were, lying in the wilderness where we must go and look for them. Spirits—I mean, images—do not come easy, not for us, at least. You have to tug at the Phantom.

16

I am trying to draw attention to the role of something hard to define in fieldwork, and that is "lived experience." It is close to what Bronislav Malinowski once called "the imponderabilia of everyday life," but he was referring to *them*, the natives, not himself, that Self he kept sealed off in his fervid diary entries that were published only after his death.

But if you want to read an account about the natives, from the exotic far away to the people next door, it seems to me you are likely to learn ever so much more if you get insight into the observer in situ as well. And isn't it required of the anthropologist intent on depicting *them* to at least try to get across the sense of life—of the observer as much as the observed? *How does it feel?* you want to know. Rarely are you told.

But is there not a problem with the depiction of lived experience and therefore with fieldwork and the fieldwork notebook today? Is not the ability to experience jeopardized by the vertiginous realities of modernity that Kafka, for one, expressed as seasickness on dry land? Perhaps life has always been like this for many people and it has little to do with "modernity." I do not know. But the instant of high-velocity sensation that goes into *I Swear I Saw This* as the taxi rushes into the tunnel must be an example of this vertigo whereby the self-extinguishing instant, like the flare of a struck match, accentuates as loss the notion of experience as something you feel you can't get a hold of. What is experienced is the loss of experience, and even that is transitory, like what happens to your sense of things when, in answer to your question, "Why are they lying there?" the taxi driver replies, "Because it's warm in there."

My drawing was made several days after the event. It was the drawing of a moment drawn from memory—from *a* memory—because there was no way I could have drawn it except after the fact. There was no way I could have drawn it there and then in the studied manner of John Berger drawing his dead father's face or when drawing a stable, settled reality, such that there develops, he thinks, a *corporeal attachment* between the drawer and the thing being drawn.

But perhaps this is reversed when drawing something fleeting, any corporeality that emerges being not so much a consequence of the drawing process as its motivation? What I mean is that my drawing is motivated by the desire to have contact because the thing witnessed dies away as soon as it is seen. This is what Benjamin must have had in mind when he wrote, with Kafka's seasickness in mind, that "Every day the urge grows stronger to get hold of an object at very close range by way of its likeness, its reproduction."[1]

And how close is "close range"? It seems to be very close, such that seeing becomes more a matter of touching and the eye becomes an exceedingly strange piece of equipment, an organ of tactility, as with Dada performance and film in which the image "hit the spectator like a bullet . . . thus acquiring a tactile quality."[2]

Despite her cool, there is surely an element of this in Joan Didion's aside—an aside itself being a minor Dada stroke—when she writes that "It is a good idea to keep in touch, and I suppose that keeping in touch is what notebooks are all about," the point being that the notes in her notebook are themselves exemplary of Dada (the overheard remarks, the isolated facts such as the one about the amount of soot falling on New York, and so forth).[3] "What kind of magpie keeps this notebook?" she asks, and goes on to cite one of her notes recording something overheard—"*He was born the night the Titanic went down.*"[4]

"That seems a nice enough line," she adds, "and I even recall who said it, but is it not really a better line in life than it could ever be in fiction?" Coming from a writer who blends (or seem to blend) fiction with nonfiction, what are we to make of this tantalizing question (if it is a question)?

One way of thinking about it is to note how this sort of overhearing (ripped out of context and allowed to float free) is very like mishearing, which can be a whole lot more interesting and a whole lot more fun than hearing. This is the essence of Dada, mishearing being close cousin to the artful distortion that occurs with repression and shock.

My point is this: that far from splattering perception into a diffuse morass of sensation, the high-velocity speed-up and disappearance of the world into an endless tunnel of night accentuates with a cruel clarity the glimpse of things but for an instant seen.

"It hit the spectator like a bullet." In other words, a glimpse can be enough. In fact it can be more than enough. Certain things seen split-second endure, if not in memory then in the body, nested in a corporeal aura, as the magpie well knows but is nevertheless impelled to write down, a writer, after all, tugging at the Phantom. (Writers steal a march on repression as well as on Freud's mystic writing pad.) It is hard to tell whether this capsulation in memory is because of the unexpectedness of what is seen or because what is seen is forbidden to see. Here I am thinking of the scenes Freud would have us ponder, primal scenes seen and not seen in the one instant of seeing and subsequently transformed into dreams and perhaps drawings—for example, the one Freud included in his publication about the Wolf Man when, at the age of twenty seven, the Wolf Man made a drawing of his childhood dream of five white wolves with big tails seated stock-still in the tree outside his bedroom window, looking at him intently. Too intently, surmised Freud, who concluded that what the stiller-than-still action masked was furious action, as with the Wolf Man's parents making love (like wolves) with their infant son quietly watching.

"He added a drawing . . . which confirmed his description," writes Freud in what to me is a curiously uncurious remark, as it is not at all obvious why a person would feel interested or compelled to make a drawing and not just continue with the "talking cure."[5] But here we immediately run into the old problem, my problem—the *I Swear I Saw This* problem—that from the very beginning pictures in the mind, categorized as "hallucinations," saturated the talking of the "talking cure," that memorable phrase coined by the most famous patient of all, known to posterity as Anna O., forever tied to the word *hysteria*, meaning above all shocking memories lodged in the body and distorting it into some sort of signaling device or theater act (let us here recall Dada).[6]

Less enduring than the primal scene, perhaps, is the odd glimpse of a naked breast or buttock through a window or as revealed by a moving curtain, the sharp blow of a fist or the glint of a knife in the silver moonlight, the flash of a shadow across a face unable for a second to resume its masklike reserve—and of course something crazy and unsettling like people sewing each other into a nylon bag by a freeway tunnel glimpsed for a second as you speed past with cars on either side of you. Based on insights from his painter companion, Brion Gysin, William Burroughs's scrapbooks would seem especially designed to mimic and to profit from such split-second unexpected moments of being that—if I have it right—open up reality like a lever heaving up a slab of ice at the edge of the frozen river we call life.

Such moments seem to be what Benjamin had in mind when, in 1940, as his last contribution to the theory of revolution a few months before he took his own life, he suggested that "To articulate the past historically . . . means to seize hold of a memory as it flashes up at a moment of danger. Historical materialism wishes to retain that image of the past which unexpectedly appears to man singled out by history at a moment of danger."[7] What this could achieve was little short of miraculous, because if it could be held onto—and that is the catch—if it could be held onto, this could amount to a Messianic cessation of happening—"put differently, a revolutionary chance in the fight for the oppressed past."[8] So here's the question. Was I unwittingly following the demand here to retain that image of the past that unexpectedly appeared to an anthropologist singled out by history at a "moment of danger"? Of course to put it this way sounds somewhat hyped, but you get my drift.

A "moment of danger." Freud put forward the notion that in modern life, with its predilection to shock—meaning an overabundance of unexpected and powerful stimuli—we tend to process experience consciously so as to blunt or prevent it passing into the unconscious, where it would otherwise hibernate as deep memory, probably in picture form if not in the bodily distortions of the hysteric.

What moments of danger do is speed up the mystic writing pad function—with this catch. It was Freud's contention that the process of fending off shocks through conscious processing builds up a stimulus shield, like the callous on an overactive thumb. But if the shock is too great, all hell breaks loose as the defense shield crashes like the dykes in New Orleans, taking the rest of body and mind with it. This is the state of physical and mental collapse we call "shock," although none of us really know what this word "shock" means. However, adds Freud, the person who is physically wounded tends to suffer less from shock than a person without a lesion because the sexual power of the wound absorbs much of the mental trauma.[9]

Could a picture and especially making a picture in such a situation be like that too, such that we might think of the picture as a lesion on one's body—on *my* body? Only it is not exactly on the body but in the fastness of that extension of the body and mind that is one's note-book—one's fieldwork notebook—forever imperfect, forever so many false starts, forever defenseless—an experiment, after all—"put differently, a revolutionary chance in the fight for the oppressed past."

17

As long as there is still one beggar around, there will still be magic.

WALTER BENJAMIN, *THE ARCADES PROJECT*

The drawing of the woman sewing the man into a nylon bag by the urban freeway that I present is like a still life or *nature mort*, as the French call it—*dead nature*. Adorno presented a formula for this life-in-death stillness when he tried to sum up Benjamin's method as the need to become a thing in order to break with the catastrophic spell of things.[1] Is this what my drawing wants too? On the one hand, coagulation into thinghood. But on the other hand, fluidity and flight in accord with the spell that breaks the spell? Yet, I ask myself, can spells, especially a "catastrophic spell," be that easily broken, and, even more to the point, what do we end up with if we follow Adorno's formula? Do we not re-create that thingified world ("reified" world, he would say)?

I thus prefer the "fixed-explosive" image and feeling set forth by Breton, as in his photograph of a "speeding locomotive abandoned for years to the delirium of a virgin forest."[2] This would not only subscribe to the abrupt encounter of natural history with history, of prehistory with history, the virgin forest with modern technology (think of tunnels and automobiles, nylon bag as shroud), but in Benjamin's hands would amount to the "dialectic at a standstill," a "dialectical image" about to burst into "now-time" such that a new spell is created in accord with my own formula: demystification and reenchantment. After all, "As long as there is one beggar around, there will still be magic."

What I am left with is the experience that shatters experience, the lived instant, which is to say the astonishment expressed by *I Swear I Saw This*, "astonishment" being the secular expression—the physical state, not the poetry—of enchantment in a disenchanted world.

And yet this too shall pass.

For is it not the case that the astonishment I express at the people lying by the freeway is *not* felt by most people living in Medellín—indeed, by anybody anywhere in today's awful world? It is not astonishing. It is an everyday event, something to which we are inured and apparently have been for a long time.

And is this not the most basic reason for the drawing, that suffering on this scale is both ordinary and extraordinary? This is the *A-Effekt* brought to our attention by Bertolt Brecht, as with his commentary on Pieter Brueghel's painting *The Fall of Icarus*. Who really cares? The plowman plows, the fisherman fishes, the ship sails on, and Icarus's fall is comic, registered by a pair of white legs flailing in the sea into which he has just fallen.

With reference to this painting, the poet W. H. Auden writes in 1938:

> About suffering they were never wrong
> The Old Masters; how well they understood
> Its human position; how it takes place
> While someone else is eating or opening a window or just walking
>   dully along

Or, you might add, just sitting in a taxi with the driver saying they lie in the tunnel because it's warm in there.

The poem continues:

> In Breughel's *Icarus*, for instance, how everything turns away
> Quite leisurely from the disaster[3]

Yet is not the point of the poem, as much as of Brecht's commentary, that a boy falling from the sky *is* astonishing but that even more astonishing is the lack of astonishment!

So, where does that place us?

When one writes *I Swear I Saw This*, it seems that indeed the stillness of the still life has found its thing-breaking spell, breaking through into this vexed territory of the human condition ,where extraordinary suffering becomes banal—or seems to.

Or seems to. For I believe this banality is never really achieved. Instead what exists is a situation of unstable equilibrium in which amazement keeps trading places back and forth with indifference. For at any moment the abnormality of the normal can spring forth, only to die away again. That is how life is in the state of emergency. All quiet on the western front. All quiet on the surface. But a boiling cauldron below. This is what the stillness of the still life, the nature mort, is pointing to. It's not really still at all.

Oh yes! Get used to it! They say. That's life. The beggar begs. In vain.

Or the opposite—the vivid photographs of horror in the media, the stories people love to tell, eyes wide. *The Horror. The Horror*—as was once famously said in another heart of darkness, but said with a sense of succumbing to the horror and becoming godlike under the load. *Fascination of the abomination.* Or maybe just cleansed, as by that mix of pity and fear that Aristotle pointed to as regards the cathartic function of tragedy holding us in its spell so long it is at one remove from reality—like my drawing of the people by the freeway.

Not really! What is released by this drawing is not catharsis but a spewing forth of "the negative sacred" with swarms of spirits unleashed—the invisible crowd of the dead—alongside the spirits of the river and the forest, from where these displaced peasants have been driven. And now we have new spirits, those of the freeways and dark tunnels and bridges and thousands of people massacred by the paramilitaries at the behest of the rich bodies in mass graves or dumped in the Cauca and Magdalena rivers—all these spirits taking us on our maiden voyage backward in time across that river where memory festers, these rivers like the Cauca and the Magdalena that have become freeways where people sew themselves into a bag by the mouth of a tunnel because "it's warm in there." You bet it's warm in there. Nothing exudes warmth like the fermenting compost of earth and sky, mortals and divinities inhabiting the wavering shafts of light in the exhaust-filled tunnel. As spirits are wont, they take on all manner of manifestations such as that woman (if she is a woman) sewing that man into that nylon bag. As for that bag, I have to tell you that it was in reality white even though in the drawing it has an irreducibly blue outline. The blue must be a sure sign that earth and sky, mortals and divinities, are being sewn into it, along with the man, if he is indeed a man. Drawing draws it out, all this.

18

With its authority dependent on "being there," anthropologists should surely be interested in what it means to bear witness, what it means to say *I Swear I Saw This*. Their craft demands close observation, complicated or improved by what is called "participant observation," seeing from the inside as well as from the outside and translating between. Yet to "bear witness" goes beyond this, suggesting observation with an edge, participation of another order.

Primo Levi was a chemist who spent most of his life after Auschwitz working in a factory in Turin. He told the novelist Phillip Roth that what he had in mind in 1946 writing *If This Is a Man* (poorly entitled in English *Survival in Auschwitz*) was what he called "the weekly factory report." He was working in a DuPont chemical factory outside of Turin at the time he was writing the book, jotting down scraps of memory when time permitted. He told Roth that that the book was written spontaneously, "on impulse, without reflecting at all," following no plan, yet years later he says, "now that I think about it, I can see that this book is full of literature."[1] It is to my mind every inch ethnography. Levi is a published poet and his book *The Periodic Table* won a prize for the best science book ever written.

Writing *Survival in Auschwitz* was "an immediate and violent impulse, to the point of competing with our most elementary needs." He felt the need for "an interior liberation." Nevertheless he remained in an almost continuous depression until he died in 1987, apparently from his own hand.

The idea for this book occurred in the death camp. It grew out of the "need to tell our story to the 'rest,' to make 'the rest' participate in it." But then a weekly factory report seems hardly the best way of making the rest participate. Despite its avowedly nonliterary and what many take to be its scientific approach, does not his account strike a mystical layer, if only because of the experience it relates and the wisdom of its author?

"Meditate that this came about," reads the line of the short poem at the front of the book, "carve its words in your heart at all times and places in the routine of the days," and then:

> Repeat them to your children,
>> Or may your house fall apart,
>> May illness impede you,
>> May your children turn their faces from you.

This is to curse. "Or may your house fall apart . . ." This is to swear *I Swear I Saw This.*

This is also quite likely to be a rewriting of the Jewish prayer, the *shema*, recited on waking and before going to bed, as one's last words, and for parents to teach to their children before going to sleep at night.[2] But while that prayer—so central to the Jewish faith—serves to swear loyalty to God, Levi has no God, not after the Lager. After the death of God there is no religion. But there is poetry and there is magic, the magic of the curse.

Seventeen years later, Levi wrote about the shame of bearing witness (although this statement was only published in 1986, a year before he died). He recalls the look on the faces of the four young Russian soldiers on horseback who rescued him that January day of snow and corpses in 1945. "They did not greet us nor did they smile," writes Levi. "They seemed oppressed not only by compassion but by a confused restraint, which sealed their lips and bound their eyes to the funereal scene."[3]

"It was that shame we knew so well," he goes on to write, the shame that during the lifespan of the camp overcame the prisoners after the guards had selected those who would be marched to the death chamber. It was the shame "that the just man experiences at another's crime, the feeling of guilt that such a crime should exist, that it should have been introduced irrevocably into the world of things that exist, and that his will for good should have proved too weak or null, and should not have availed in defense."[4] He feels that his having survived disqualifies him as a witness because only the cunning and the ruthless survived. Yet we have his book, do we not, a book of witness? "Meditate that this came about."

I recall what I was told around 1980 by a Colombian anthropologist who asked some Huitoto Indians along the lower reaches of the Putumayo River in Colombia about the atrocities of the rubber boom made famous in 1911 in Europe and North America by the British consul Roger Casement. The Indians responded by asking the anthropologist a question: "Why do you want to know about such things? Only sorcerers want to know this because they use such stories to do evil." True, false, or in between, this story has weighed on me to the present, for it suggests that as regards atrocity there is wisdom in muteness and that to bear witness to atrocity requires particular measures and conditions that could indeed be regarded as magical.

Levi has little patience with the mute option, if option it be. When a prominent literary critic, such as George Steiner, declares that "Auschwitz lies outside speech," or Adorno advises that "to write poetry after Auschwitz is barbaric," Levi flatly disagrees, as his poem, which is a curse, on the first page of his book of witness testifies. He regards the mute option as a common misperception.[5] From his interview with Philip Roth it seems he found his polar star to steer by in the driest possible presentation one could conceive of, that of the factory report, unemotional in tone but not in impact.[6] Auschwitz was a factory (and we might recall the term "factory" given to the depots on the West African coast for holding slaves prior to export to the New World), but there was this difference: its product was death and its constituents were people. Yet to do justice to that experience—the human, in its inhumanity—the factory report was not enough. What it provided, however, was that magical armature the Huitotos in my story implied was necessary.

Is my drawing such a magical measure? Is it a response to the shame to which Primo Levi refers, in despite of which he writes? Possibly. But there has to be one proviso; that the stupendous abnormality of what Levi lived through is all too absent in the stupendous normality of the abnormal in daily life in today's third-world cities. It is this normality of the abnormal, the fact that the state of emergency is not the exception but the rule, that this drawing of mine is getting at. Why are they lying down by the tunnel? "Because it is warm in there."

Levi would understand. He belongs to no recognizable school. Although Jewish and at least partly educated in a Jewish school in Turin, he abjures religion just as he does psychology or psychoanalysis in relation to the events he relates. If anything, he belongs to Benjamin's storyteller, who abjures explanation altogether.

19

More self than one's self, this ancillary organ called the fieldwork notebook plots a course between chance and story. Lying here in the dark at 5:30 AM, writing in my notebook one week after my drive through the tunnel in Medellin. I feel warm and enclosed. I can hear a slight drizzle outside, radio news crackling, footsteps outside on the pebble-covered path. No cars, no electricity. No exhaust. No TV. The bedspread is embroidered with beautiful blue flowers, the delicacy of which stands in such vivid contrast to the workaday reality here of mud and rain. The flowers are the same color as I have painted the nylon bag into which the woman by the freeway is sewing that man. I too am being sewn into my cocoon. There is a slit of light coming through the wooden window shutter. I feel an immense and beautiful calm, a calm that may not last but feels as if it could. I think of the people here as "still honest," as William says when he sells on credit from his tiny shop, confident—or at least hopeful—that one day he will be paid back. I think of how little people have here, yet how cheerily they set about the day, how elegant they are, how immense their labor. But I have to leave that beautiful bedspread even though I have only just arrived.

The guerrilla are close by in the forest. I can stay only one night. The army ambushed the guerrilla here on Easter, when they went swimming in the river, and I am told they will be back to take revenge on people they think gave the army information. William will take me downstream in the dugout canoe in an hour. Once a mighty tree, it now encloses us securely as we slip through the mist in the dawn.

The youngest kid in this household is about five years old and is called Don King, which sounds like a musical gong has been struck when you say it in Spanish with the accentuation over the first and second *n*. His sister Wendy Zulay gave him this name. This morning I see him standing on the bed with a solemn face helping his sister, Liliana, with the hooks on the back of her dress.

In my notebook, Gustavo says he dreamed half a year ago that I brought him a Singer sewing machine. It was all white. He laughs. He can make a suit, he says, and learned to tailor from an auntie in Buenaventura. He doesn't have a place of his own, an *enclosure*, we might say. His temporary abode is that of a cousin who lives in Cali. It is a bare wooden building with signs of having once been lived in, but now it feels emptier than empty. There are two moldy travel bags in a corner. He says he sits all day. He is childless and never married or lived with anyone. His legs are no good for working in the river any more, searching for gold. Over the years his legs have been hammered by falling rocks. He shows me the scars. He smiles all the time and looks dashing—as always—with his elegant thinness, black trousers, bare feet, checked shirt, and a grey straw hat with an orange ribbon. When his sister, who lives opposite and provides him with meals, told him of 9/11, he tells me he cried and prayed that nothing had happened to me. The village is full of thieves, he says. They steal chickens and they steal from each other's mines. I know that he steals a lot, too, but it's more like "borrowing." He wanders in and out of everyone's house all the time, free as a bird, it seems.

Doña Lucia is here in my notebook too. Straight out of nowhere. A presence like hers is bound to make an entrance sooner or later and stand foursquare on the page in front of you with her mighty shoulders and huge straw hat to blunt the force of the rain and the sun. She is seventy-two years old and washes for gold in the river every day, as well as being an expert healer of *ojo* and *espanto*. Her movements are exquisite and convincing. *Ojo* means evil eye. *Espanto* is fright. The way she stands over the prone patient, a child, she looks just like she is panning for gold in the river, bent at the hips with her legs straight. Actually she is using eight-year-old Liliana as a model. She measures Liliana's waist, folds the string into quarters, then, holding each end firmly in each hand, makes her way up the child, length by length, from foot to crown. She measures the waist again. This time there is a discrepancy, a gap of one finger's width. "The child is *un dedo espantado!*—one finger's width inflicted with *espanto*."

She folds the string into quarters again and this time zigzags down from head to foot. This will close the *espanto*. She measures the waist again to see if she has succeeded. She admits that she can't cure a gap greater than four *dedos*.

All the time she is silently praying a special prayer. Later she asks if I want to learn it. She will sell it to me. I think of Gustavo and his chickens.

Liliana's mother, Lilia—who embroidered those beautiful blue flowers on my bedspread—tells me more about *espanto*, to which children are so susceptible. Children startle easy, in their sleep, for instance. For kids have visions, especially kids who cannot speak. They see the dead and they see strange spirits, and in such a state, or simply by being capable of such a state, they are vulnerable to *espanto*, meaning "fright."

I draw a drawing of the homeless by the freeway as a measure of control and as a way of marking what I have witnessed. Doña Lucia measures the body of the witness traumatized by a vision of the other world, and then she uses her measuring instrument to close the body, so long as the gap is four *dedos* or less. She uses a secret prayer as well. She solicits forces similar to those she wants to back off. But, then, don't we all have such a prayer?

I Swear I Saw This.

Afterthoughts are what I call the notes you feel impelled to write in your fieldwork diary a few hours or days after a diary entry. Naturally, I am talking of handwriting, an ancient technology that allows the pen to slide away from forming letters and words to form pictures and back again to words. You start in the margin next to the relevant entry and end up God knows where, perhaps right here at the end of a book about drawings in fieldwork notebooks, namely my own. Spurred on by that earlier entry, or rather its felt incompleteness, afterthoughts add layers to that entry, imageric and meditative. Afterthoughts often seem the most important aspect about an event that for some reason hadn't occurred to you when writing because of writing, another manifestation of the mystic writing pad hitched to the Phantom. Such retrieval is irritating. Why does it have to be this way? Why can't things be more straightforward? What gives with this crazy montage (I was going to say "marriage") combining writing and thoughts that surge later, much later? Why is it that the uninscribed requires the banal everyday set down until that time when afterthoughts fly in like sparrows in the late afternoon, and you can, along with Joan Didion, go the whole hog and tug and tug at that Phantom for all it's worth?

And now with these afterthoughts unfolding, I see how strange the whole thing has become. On the one hand, so long as there is life there is no end to afterthoughts. At the same time, however, the notebook from which they originate supplies not only the energy but also the material for such splendid fireworks. For has not this very book, *I Swear I Saw This*, a silent partner, namely the notebook of August

2006 for which this book before you is but an incandescent afterthought? The notebook supplies the there there.

The relationship between past and present unfolding here is somewhat more complicated and interesting than being dragged if not drugged into a stepwise succession of associations, a spider's web of traceries. Like those grids that so fascinated Brion Gysin, supposedly arising from the juxtaposition of Japanese script (vertical) with Arabic script (horizontal), the writing in a diary glides from present to present like a hawk on the wing. This "presentism" is one of the most exciting features in such writing, as if the lived moment is pressed still hot onto a photosensitive plate. But at the same time a "vertical" dimension asserts itself into every word and phrase, not only after, as the phrase "afterthoughts" suggests, but very much in the present too, as if there can be no present without its pastness. This one learns, this one sees quickly in writing in a diary. Or is it a notebook?

As I pondered the drawing of the people by the freeway tunnel, I came to realize that this book would be about seeing as witnessing in relation to fieldnotes and that the *book* needed to parallel the *notebook*, to share the way by which that one drawing meshed with the chronology beginning with the shock of the freeway tunnel in Medellin and ending in a village surrounded by guerrilla in the jungle of the Pacific coast where an old healer is demonstrating to me the art of healing *espanto*, an illness affecting young children of whom I now see I must be one.

That ending, healing *espanto*, was pure caprice. Out of the blue it came at me as something that seemed just right, the tone and the feel as much as anything else. I saw it as a reprieve, a slow letting go, a slow farewell to writing a book, slipping into the dugout, slipping downstream in the early morning mist. I wanted an aura of facticity to rise at the end like that rising mist, and even more than the aura of facticity I wanted the book to mirror the staggered realism of a notebook, jumping from one apparently unrelated incident to the next like a butterfly from flower to flower.

The facticity was meant to convey the grit and grain of note taking as raw description, which of course is never all that raw but has at least a hint of poetry reaching out to the mystery of the great unknown. That raw facticity with its motley array of things (for example, William's store, Don King, and Gustavo's chickens) like the interior of a dresser drawer was my underhand way of saying, "Look, here is the notebook once again, emerging from the shadows if only for an instant, taking its curtain call!" It was partly by design that I did this, but also by chance, mirroring the role of chance in fieldwork but here applied to writing—which is why I want to insist on the correspondence between fieldwork and writingwork which, in this instance, at least, provides a rather nice example of the cut-up principle as well—with the magic that implies.

A cut-up is collage applied not only to images only, but to writing as well. A cut-up is a surprise, for it consists of apparently incongruous parts that are almost brutal in their juxtaposition—as the name "cut-up" implies. But there is something in this mad mix that hits the eye and lifts the soul, and it is this combustible mix of congruousness within incongruity that does the work.

Yet is not fact stranger than fiction? The art of the cut-up is there staring you in the face in everyday life. So why don't we see it that way? Is that the mystic writing pad working overtime? Poor thing.

When Brion Gysin got turned onto magic in a practical sort of way, it was in Tangiers in 1958 through his finding a sorcery packet—let us call it a cut-up, where the art of such meets the everydayness of such— the size of a cigarette pack hidden in the fan housing of the ventilator of the club he owned, called The 1001 Nights, which he had created so as to be able to listen to the spellbinding music of the master musicians of the mountain village of Jajouka, whom he got to play in the club every one of those 1,001 nights. The sorcery worked. Gysin lost his club, but the sorcery worked apotropaically to his benefit as well, containing a magical grid that set in motion a revolution in twentieth-century art-making.

The sorcery packet contained the following facts:

- seven seeds
- seven shards of mirror
- seven speckled pebbles
- two fingernail-sized pieces of carved lead, one the head of a bull, the other a profile of Brion Gysin
- a square of paper bearing "a cabbalistic spell," which was meant to be read with the paper held one way, and then read another way to "lock the meaning in"[1]

Whereas in my case the magic cut-up began with a drawing counterbalanced with an ending placed penultimately at the end before the end in a small village at the end of a river studded with facticity, where a healer is healing *espanto*, an illness caused by witnessing the untoward, the central concern of *I Swear I Saw This*.

To be studded with facticity, like stars in the firmament, is the same as the collation of seven seeds and seven mirrors, a bull's head, and, of course, a likeness of the author. To stud with facticity is to recognize that writing can produce spells, too, and reading even more so.

This is given in the nature of fieldwork and hence its notebooks— No! let's change that; *because of its notebooks*—and because of the special type of *knowing* that fieldwork creates, experiential and interactional, based on the relationship between observer and observed, guest and host, such that any claim to accuracy requires the observer observed, which is easier said than done. As for experience, or what is sometimes referred to as "lived experience," this is more than the facts that can be distilled from a situation, although everything here depends on how we define a fact. You can see facts as marbles, like atoms or coins, which is what social science does, or you can see facts like those speckled marbles in the ventilator shaft of The 1001 Nights. Read *Ulysses* by James Joyce, a book about a man frying kidneys for breakfast, thinking about his ladylove upstairs and the cat rubbing his leg. And that was a book covering a mere twenty-four hours of the observer observed. The kidneyness of the kidney is that singular fact that explodes facticity.

What is more, fieldwork and hence its notebooks produce a knowing that is largely the result of stories and chance embedded in what could be called the "stranger effect," whereby the anthropologist-observer is credited with mysterious power no less than with childlike ignorance and vulnerability. This mysterious power is also connected to but not necessarily the same as that of the state or the occupying power or the upper classes or a white skin, no matter how much the anthropologist disapproves. But that is not all. Not by a long shot. The anthropologist is quintessentially a stranger in a foreign land asking for directions and, in the process, likely to be changed in some fundamental way. We could think of the great story in anthropology as how such a change is dealt with, whether it is recognized, and how it is acted upon in the rest of the anthropologist's life until death. Yet that story remains largely untold, although there are hopeful signs of cracks in that edifice.[2] The discipline of anthropology sterilizes all of that like a catalytic convertor depolluting car exhaust.

As for the story-laden character of anthropological knowledge and hence its notebooks, is it not the ultimate betrayal to render stories as "information" and not as stories? The first problem with this is that it is rarely realized or appreciated by anthropologists that most of what they are told comes in the form of a story. Because of their training and professional culture, they are too often insensitive to this basic feature of experience. It is like being colorblind or, worse still, actually blind. The next step in this betrayal is the instant translation of the story into a fact, or what is called "data," and along with that the storyteller is translated into an "informant." Once these steps have been achieved (and the process is rapid-fire and unconscious), the philosophical character of the knowing is changed. The reach and imagination in the story is lost.

If not told a story, the anthropologist frequently inhabits one. When I record how I met two young field hands one late afternoon coming home from work, slowly dancing to music from a transistor radio hung on the crossbar of their bike, their long shadows undulating in the dust, not a word was passed between us. It was like a dream image. That, too, is to inhabit the story, and to inhabit the story is to allow an image, like a shadow dancing in the dust, to encircle us all.

I find myself thinking a lot about these "moments" that erupt from nowhere, it seems. They slow things down, an oasis in the desert Genet talks about, like a drawing in the middle of pages of furious writing. The "moments" are imageric and come at the point where a story morphs into a picture, which must be how history is made and unmade and why—without knowing or caring why—I made my drawings. I have a picture of a peasant field in my head and maybe in a notebook, too. I saw the field from a bus window up high on a causeway. There was a zigzag path running through it. I see it clearly. It keeps coming back. All I have to do is press the button, by which I mean write. Here it comes.

I see five or six people sitting on benches with empty bottles of *aguardiente* in front of them. It is a tiny country store with a cement slab and a crude roof under which an old toothless couple are dancing slowly, smooth as silk, as the sun drops. Two old women, skinny as reeds, are dancing with each other too. The owner of the store leans out over a half door, acting as DJ. Another moment. Another button pressed. The dark beyond the plantains, the scars of poverty and hardship on the faces, the grace of movement that the space they made opens out.

Through the iron grill that secures the front door, I watch the street outside get darker. The wall of the house on the other side of the street goes gray, then fades into blackness. A solitary woman walks by fast. In a soft voice as soft as her blouse, Gloria tells me that we cannot talk of the assassinations occurring daily, the *limpieza*.

Another button, the ephemera of the everyday as in the fieldwork diary, facts scattered like the corn seed thrown either side as we walk that zigzag path.

No agribusiness writing here.

Can a fact like a kidney be a story, and if so, what sort of story? A modern story, perhaps, like Joan Didion's "FACT"—during 1964, 720 tons of soot fell on every square mile of New York City[3]—or like Charles Olson's *Call Me Ishmael*, a book about Herman Melville and Moby Dick. Just look at the table of contents. Just pull at the Phantom.

FIRST FACT is prologue.
Then comes:
part 1 is FACT.

Here the accentuation of fact in capital letters brings out the fact that a fact like the anthropologist inhabiting her story is capacious and habitable when seen from the appropriate angle or, should I say, from within the appropriate circle. A fact is, you might say, a modern story. But then it is very ancient too. Take the example from Herodotus that Walter Benjamin supplies in his famous essay on the storyteller.[4] Could there be anything more dry, factual, and free of explanation than the description of the conquered king forced to witness his captive children and servant in the victory march of his enemies, weeping only when he sees the servant? Take Primo Levi.

So far I may seem to have assumed that there is a basic story form and that we all know and agree on what that is. But that is absurd.

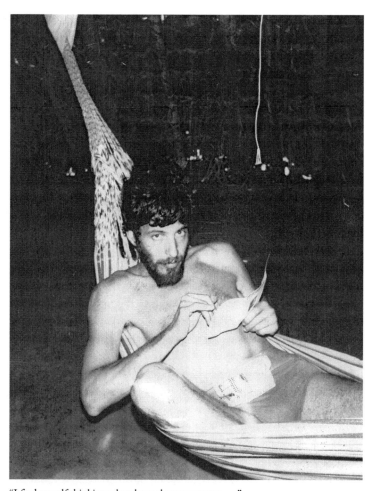

"I find myself thinking a lot about these moments . . ."

I have simplified so as to draw out the contrast with other forms of speech and writing that are generally seen as anything but stories, such as that produced by most historians and anthropologists, for whom a story is way down on the totem pole of truthifying. And I have simplified because of the problem that runs across all the others and that is the impossibility of cleanly separating fiction from nonfiction or from what we call documentary. What we mean by "story" swarms across this boundary—and no wonder, because while that boundary is one of the most fundamental ways by which we fix and figure reality, it is actually porous and, not to be too cute, a lively piece of fiction itself. This is why style and voice are so important, for it is they that do the heavy lifting of analysis.

Swarming. By the early 1980s I was creating fieldwork notebooks combining my private life with public worlds along with a whole lot more sensitivity to supernatural experience, such as sorcery. (I mean, come on! I grew up in a nice bohemian headland in Sydney, where the kids go barefoot and nobody bothers with church.) These notebooks were in synch with Dada-like impulsions combining sorcery with its hallucinogenic healing, as sung by my healer friend Santiago Mutumbajoy, whom I visited year in and year out in the Colombian Putumayo from 1975 to 1997.

As the violence in Colombia and the world grew worse and the rumor mill in the media and on the street created ever more "multiple realities," basic to terror, I see that I was pasting more and more clippings from newspapers and magazines into my notebooks. So what started off in 1969 when I first arrived in Colombia as two cardboard boxes with files of notes organized by categories such as "land tenure," "Church," and so on became instead an ongoing series of notebooks filled with spasmodic streams of bric-a-brac.

I would say it was the discovery of *multiple realities* as long ago as 1980 that really did me in. This was the Great Turning Point. You can get a sense of it by reading Gabriel García Márquez's book *Chronicle of a Death Foretold*, with its penumbra of fate playing out step by step amid swirling rumor and multiangled perspectives. I woke up to this multiple-realities thing first when asking different people about the miracles that gave rise to the saints in the different churches around where I was living in the south of the Cauca Valley. Just about everybody I asked gave me a different account. Later there were the corpses found every few days or weeks on the sides of the roads leading into town. Everyone had a different story to tell about what seemed indisputably one and the same thing.

In my little corner of that world, I came to realize that there were almost as many accounts of the untoward—saints and corpses—as there were people with whom I spoke, including myself. There is an expression I heard a few times in Colombia, "Each head is a world." It did not fit in with my view of society. There was an edge to it that made me wonder. My basic assumption that society is built on a pretty substantial block of agreement about what is going on was being threatened. But the truly critical lesson was this: until then my assumption was that my task as an anthropologist was to sift through this rampant heterogeneity and find the truth, whether it be the average, the "standard distribution," the majority, or that peculiar animal called "the underlying." But now that all seemed simplistic, vacuous, and missing the point that it was this very multiplicity of difference along with its associated fragmentation that was reality. What I am saying here may sound terribly obvious—but, believe me, it was not what I was hearing in the halls of academe with regard to the assumptions of social inquiry.

Here is where reality as *cut-up* helped me a lot. In adhering to a date line, as with a diary, in juxtaposing (but not supplanting) order with disorder, and text with image, what I construed as a scrapbook picked up on strange trails of memory and layered afterthoughts that, in mimicking the push and pull of reality, had a fighting chance of outwitting what I came to call The Nervous System (NS), by which I meant reality as a state of emergency, confounding order with disorder and vice versa before you could wink an eye.

What this amounts to is the same play with chance and fate that goes on in what Benjamin called a "genuine" collection. Here the collection is what is in the notebook or, to be more precise, what goes on in rereading and spinning afterthoughts. It is this same play of order and disorder, this same locking horns of fate with chance, that defines sorcery and its cure.

All of which puts our intellectual work in a new light. Whether that is art or science I do not know, but one thing needs to be made clear. If Burroughs and Gysin assumed they were artists, bent on transforming the grounds of experience and hence the world, carefully selecting each image and each particle of prose to make up each scrapbook page, my task was quite different because I was far more bound by the demands of keeping a record than making a page that could emit occult power. Yet it is undeniable that as the fetish power of the notebook grew—that fetish that becomes more self than oneself with its own intense, aesthetic demands—so did its occult power, combined with the chance-effects of afterthoughts as you pulled at the Phantom.

All along I had an image in mind. I was thinking of what it was like when you approached those military checkpoints on the road through the mountain passes of the Andes down to Mocoa, once Julio César Turbay Ayala, *el Turco*, then president of Colombia, invoked a state of emergency, giving the army free rein to do whatever the hell they wanted after the M-19 guerrilla made them look stupid, stealing their weapons by tunneling into the dark mountain, itself like a cutout, rearing up into the blue sky behind Bogotá, New Year's Eve 1979. They left a note: *Año Nuevo y Armas Nuevas*. Happy New Year and Happy New Arms. Humor is the lover of the NS, just as humor is only a cat's whisker removed from violence.

Checkpoints. Check your points. What a mighty amalgam of fact and figure of speech are checkpoints, magnification of the barriers we encounter in the round of everyday life. On the one hand, this crossing to the other side was all about rules and order, the very magic of the state. But when you complied with that, you soon discovered how wrong you were. Now it was all about exceptions to order. So you tacked back and forth to their questions and nasty faces, always one step behind, unbalanced and awkward. After all, this tacking back and forth was what you had gotten accustomed to do writing, then reading and rereading your notes in your notebook, daily assuming more fearsome, more lovable fetish status. Here again was the Nervous System, the nervously nervous Nervous System. And it was the same experience trying in vain to get a Venezuelan visa on the border with Colombia by the Guajira peninsula east of Rio Hacha, pillaged by Drake in 1596 looking for pearls and gold. Through the slit in the dark glass, all you could see was a mobile Bolivarian moustache like some undersea clam opening and closing on its prey. The whole point of power is its ability to change not only the rules midstream, but the aesthetic of flows and rhythms. This one learns early in life but holds at arm's length as too scary or too complicated so that you allow the great tropes of order to hold sway, whether in religion, ritual, politics, or narrative. Yet surely scrutiny of any situation teaches otherwise, that early in life was right and that Nervous System aesthetics underlie all of life and not just its early perceptions.

I attributed agency to the NS. I understood it as possessed of a will and mind of its own. The moment you recognized that indeterminacy was the rule of the game, the damn thing, the NS, would snap back at you and proclaim order as regnant. And the moment you went the other direction—Aha! Now I get it: order, structure, hierarchy and all those good things, that's what I should be after—then it would revert to its earlier position, leaving you floundering. It is as if the NS can sense your moves before they happen and act accordingly. The point then is to figure out a craft—or is it an art?—for how to get the jump on such a demonic reality that preemptively twists and turns in response to your attempts to get a hold of it before it gets a hold of you. This is why I like the idea of fieldnotes with their afterthoughts chasing first thoughts, then second thoughts, ad infinitum through the sieve of derealization that writing creates in a cascade of scribbles that no NS can contain while you tug at the Phantom that, in the guise of a drawing, refuses to give the NS its fix.

ACKNOWLEDGMENTS

Chris Bracken showed me what I was doing but didn't know I was doing. María del Rosario Ferro and I discussed what fieldwork writing was and could be, as we both scribbled away side by side in Puerto Tejada and on the Sierra Nevada. Stephen Muecke and Daniella Gandolfo added to my sense of the magic of chance, as did Laura Hoptman when she invited me to speak about her great exhibition on Brion Gysin at the New Museum in New York. Therese Davis in Melbourne, David Levi-Strauss in New York, and Claudia Steiner in Bogotá provided great venues for discussing drawings in fieldwork notebooks with a motley crew of film critics, visual artists, performance artists, writers, and anthropologists. As concept and argument, Tom Mitchell's "picture theory" gave wings to my wondering, why draw and not write? Olivia Mostacilla and Luís Carlos Mina of Puerto Tejada seem there on every page of my notebooks, as do Lilia Zuñiga, William Amú, their daughter Liliana, and Gustavo Cesbén, residents of Santa María up the Timbiquí River. Santiago Mutumbajoy's singing in the Putumayo night haunts me always, despite my clownish drawings of those nights. Many thanks (what an understatement!) to Simryn Gill for her gift of the Walter Benjamin pearls and to Carmen Albers for her giraffe. A grant from the Ruth Landes Memorial Foundation enabled me to finish. Matt Keyes and my animator daughter Olivia photoshopped the images. Marielle Nitoslawska and Nancy Goldring were in this project from the start, providing both wind and keel until we arrived in port.

NOTES

CHAPTER ONE

1. Daniel Wilkinson, "Death and Drugs in Colombia," *New York Review of Books*, August 18, 2011.
2. Juan Forero, "As Colombian War Crimes Suspects Sit in U.S. Jails, Victims' Kin Protest," *Washington Post*, October 5, 2009. See also "17 Soacha Perpetrators Are Free," cip-colombia-news@googlegroups.com, January 9, 2010.
3. Jeremy McDermott, "Toxic Fallout of Colombian Scandal," BBC News, http://news.bbc.co.uk/2/hi/americas/8038399.stm, May 8, 2009.
4. Derek Attridge, "Roland Barthes's Obtuse, Sharp Meaning and the Responsibilities of Commentary," in *Writing The Image After Roland Barthes*, ed. Jean-Michel Rabaté (Philadelphia: University of Pennsylvania Press, 1997), 79.
5. Roland Barthes, "The Third Meaning: Research Notes on Some Eisenstein Stills," in *A Barthes Reader*, ed. Susan Sontag (New York: Hill and Wang, 1982), 318.
6. Jean Genet, *Prisoner of Love* (New York: New York Review of Books, 2003).
7. Walter Benjamin, "Surrealism," in *Reflections: Essays, Aphorisms, Autobiographical Writings* (New York: Schocken, 1986), 182–83.
8. Benjamin, "Surrealism," 183.

CHAPTER TWO

1. *New York Times*, October 26, 2007, A4. See also Christina Thompson, "Smoked Heads," in *The Best Australian Essays: 2006*, ed. Drusilla Modjeska (Melbourne: Black, 2006), 23–37.
2. Roland Barthes, "Deliberation," in *A Barthes Reader*, ed. Susan Sontag (New York: Hill and Wang, 1982), 494, 495.
3. Roland Barthes, "One Always Fails in Speaking of What One Loves," in *The Rustle of Language* (Oxford: Basil Blackwell, 1986), 296–308.
4. Ibid., 301.

5. Ibid., 304–5.
6. Sigmund Freud, "A Note upon the 'Mystic Writing-Pad,'" in *The Standard Edition of the Complete Psychological Works of Sigmund Freud* (Richmond: Hogarth Press and the Institute of Psycho-Analysis, 1968), 19:227–32.
7. Simon Ottenberg, "Thirty Years of Fieldnotes: Changing Relationsips to the Text," *Fieldnotes: The Makings of Anthropology*, ed. Roger Sanjek (Ithaca: Cornell University Press, 1990), 139–60.
8. Joan Didion, "On Keeping a Notebook," in *Slouching Towards Bethlehem* (New York: Farrar Strauss Giroux, 1968), 131–41.
9. Walter Benjamin, "Theses on the Philosophy of History," in *Illuminations* (New York: Shocken, 1968), 253–64.

CHAPTER THREE

1. John Berger, *A Seventh Man* (New York: Viking Adult, 1975), and John Berger, *Ways of Seeing* (Boston; Penguin, 1990).
2. John Berger, "John Berger, Life Drawing," in *Berger on Drawing*, ed. Jim Savage (London: Occasional Press, 2007), 3.
3. Benjamin, "On the Mimetic Faculty," in *Reflections*, 333.
4. Christopher Grubbs, "Drawing Life, Drawing Ideas," in *Drawing/Thinking: Confronting an Elextronic Age*, ed. Marc Treib (New York: Routledge, 2008), 105.
5. "Distance and Drawings: Four Letters from the Correspondence between James Elkins and John Berger," in *Berger on Drawing*, ed. Jim Savage (Aghabullogue: Occasional Press, 2007), 106, 108.
6. Ibid., 116.
7. See the essay by Anthony Dubovsky, "The Euphoria of the Everyday," Treib, *Drawing/Thinking*, 72–81; see esp. 75.
8. Jacques Derrida, *Memoirs of the Blind: The Self-Portrait and Other Ruins* (Chicago: University of Chicago Press, 1993), 4–5.
9. Chip Sullivan, "Telling Untold Stories," in Treib, *Drawing/Thinking*, 122–35; see esp. 132.
10. "Drawn to that Moment," in Savage, *Berger on Drawing*.
11. Jean Jackson, "'I Am A Fieldnote': Fieldnotes a a Symbol of Professional Identity," in Sanjek, *Fieldnotes*, 30.
12. Ibid., 29.
13. Ibid., 28.
14. Ibid., 29.
15. Laura Bohannan [Eleanor Smith Bowen, pseud.], *Return to Laughter: An Anthropological Novel* (New York: Doubleday and the American Museum of Natural History, 1954).
16. Ibid., 165–66.
17. Ibid., 30, 34.
18. Ibid., 213.
19. Ibid., 229.

20. Ibid., 289.
21. Ibid., 291.
22. Ibid., 57.
23. Benjamin, "The Storyteller," in *Illuminations*, 91.
24. Ibid., 109.
25. Bohannan, *Return to Laughter* 70.

CHAPTER FOUR

1. See Wendy Gunn, ed., *Fieldnotes and Sketchbooks* (Frankfurt: Peter Land, 2009).
2. Lynn Gumpert, "From Concept to Object: The Artistic Practice of Drawing," in Trieb *Thinking/Drawing*, 46–59; see esp. 46.
3. Laurie Olin, "More Than Rigging Your Wrist (or Your Mouse): Thinking, Seeing, and Drawing," in Trieb, *Drawing/Thinking*, 82.
4. Julie Bosman, "Picture Books, Long a Staple, Lose Out in the Rush to Read," *New York Times*, October 8, 2010, A1, A15.
5. Roald Hoffmann, *The Same and Not the Same* (New York: Columbia University Press, 1997), 69. Todd Ochoa put me on to this.
6. Melanie Holcomb, *Pen and Parchment: Drawing in the Middle Ages* (New York: Metropolitan Museum of Art, 2009), 31–33. Many thanks to Nancy Goldring for this reference
7. Holcomb, *Pen and Parchment*, 31.
8. See the catalog of the meticulously assembled exhibition at the New Museum, New York City, curated by Laura Hoptman in 2010, especially her essay, "Disappearing Act: The Art of Brion Gysin" (New York: New Museum, 2010), 57–143. Also William S. Burroughs and Robert A. Sobieszek, *Ports of Entry: William S. Burroughs and the Arts* (Los Angeles: Los Angeles County Museum of Art, 1996), 45–53.
9. See frequent references to orgasm (especially from the hung corpse) in Burroughs's later works and in Brion Gysin, interviewed by Terry Wilson, *Here to Go: Planet R-101* (San Francisco: Re/Search Publications, 1982), 62.
10. Gysin and Wilson, *Here to Go*, 76
11. Brion Gysin, *The Process* (New York: Doubleday, 1969), 65–66.
12. Gysin in Gysin and Wilson, *Here to Go*, 187.
13. Gysin and Wilson, *Here to Go*, 167.
14. William Burroughs, *Cities of the Red Night* (New York: Henry Holt, 1981), 27.
15. Ibid., 91.
16. Ibid., 93.
17. Ibid., 103.
18. Ibid., 142.
19. Barry Miles, *A Descriptive Catalogue of the William S. Burroughs Archive* (New York; Covent Garden Press, 1974), 79.
20. Gysin in Gysin and Wilson, *Here to Go*, 50.

CHAPTER FIVE

1. James Agee, *Let Us Now Praise Famous Men* (New York: Houghton Mifflin, 1939 [1940]), 8.
2. William S. Burroughs, "William S. Burroughs, The Art of Fiction No. 36," interview by Conrad Knickerbocker, *Paris Review* 35 (Fall 1965).
3. Mateo Mina, *Esclavitud y libertad en el Valle del rio Cauca* (Bogota: La Rosca, 1975).
4. Cf. Walter Benjamin, *The Origin of German Tragic Drama* (London: New Left Books, 1977), 92.

CHAPTER SIX

1. Brion Gysin, "Cut-Ups: A Project for Disastrous Success," in William S. Burroughs and Brion Gysin, *The Third Mind* (New York: Viking), 1978), 42.
2. Brion Gysin, interviewed by Terry Wilson, *Here to Go: Planet R-101* (San Francisco: Re/Search Publications, 1982), 234.
3. Brion Gysin, interviewed by Terry Wilson, *Here to Go: Planet R-101* (San Francisco: Re/Search Publications, 1982), 234.
4. Gysin, "Cut-Ups," in Burroughs and Gysin, *The Third Mind*, 42–43.
5. William S. Burroughs, *Queer* (Boston: Penguin, 1987), xiii.
6. Antonin Artaud, "Concerning a Journey to the Land of the Tarahumaras: The Mountain of Signs," in *Antonin Artaud Anthology*, ed. Jack Hirschman (San Francisco: City Lights, 1965), 69.
7. Vincent Crapanzano emphasizes the importance of chance in his essay "At The Heart of the Discipline," *Emotions in the Field: The Psychology and Anthropology of Field Experience*, ed. in James Davies and Dimitrina Spencer (Stanford: Stanford University Press, 2010), 60–61. Writing on what he calls "the importance of the contingent and accidental in fieldwork," he notes that "I know of no anthropologist who has not recounted the contingencies that led him or her to settle in a particular village, live with a certain family, meet an especially insightful informant, or discover an aspect of the society or culture hitherto unknown to him or her. I myself could give countless examples."
8. Laura Bohannan, "Hamlet in the Bush."
9. Also see Stephen Muecke and Max Pam, *Contingency in Madagascar* (Bristol: Intellect Books, 2011).
10. Daisy Tan Dic Sze, "A Taste for Ethics: Shifting from Lifestyle to Way of Life" (PhD dissertation, Goldsmiths College, University of London, 2009), 54.
11. Daniella Gandolfo, *The City at Its Limits: Taboo, Transgression, and Urban Renewal in Lima* (Chicago: University of Chicago Press, 2009), xi, xii.
12. Nick Paumgarten, "Acts of God," *New Yorker*, July 12–19, 2010, 30–31.
13. Friedrich Nietzsche, *On The Genealogy of Morals*, trans. Walter Kauffman (Vintage: New York), 69.

14. William Burroughs, *The Western Lands* (New York: Viking Penguin, 1987), 113.
15. E. E. Evans Pritchard, *Witchcraft, Oracle, and Magic among the Azande* (Oxford: Oxford University Press, 1937), 193.
16. Taussig, "Viscerality, Faith, and Skepticism, Another Theory of Magic," in. *Defacement.*

CHAPTER SEVEN

1. Denis Holier, ed., *The College of Sociology* (Minneapolis: University of Minnesota Press, 1988 [1979]).
2. Frank G. Speck, *Naskapi: The Savage Hunters of the Labrador Peninsula* (Norman: University of Oklahoma Press, 9178), 210–20.
3. Alejo Carpentier, prologue to *The Kingdom of This World*, trans. Harriet de Onís (New York: Farrar, Straus and Giroux, 1972).
4. Ludwig Wittgenstein, *Remarks on Frazer's "Golden Bough,"* ed. Rush Rhees (Atlantic Highlands, NJ: Humanities Press, 1979).
5. Juan Rulfo, *Pedro Paramo* (1955; repr., Madrid: Editorial Debate, 2000), 8–9.

CHAPTER EIGHT

1. Walter Benjamin, "Surrealism: Last Snapshot of the European Intelligentsia," in *Reflections*, 189–90. "For histrionic or fanatical stress on the mysterious side of the mysterious takes us no further; we penetrate the mystery only to the degree that we recognize it in the everyday world, by virtue of a dialectical optic that perceives the everyday as impenetrable, the impenetrable as everyday."
2. Georges Bataille, *Prehistoric Painting, Lascaux, or the Birth of Art* (Geneva: Skira, 1955), 14–15.
3. Georges Bataille, *The Accursed Share: An Essay on General Economy Consumption* (1976; repr., New York: Zone Books, 1991), 209.
4. Brion Gysin, *To Master—A Long Goodnight: The Story of Uncle Tom, A Historical Narrative* (New York: Creative Age Press, 1949), 121.
5. Wittgenstein, *Remarks on Frazer's "Golden Bough."*

CHAPTER NINE

1. Celine Sparrow, email, December 14, 2008.
2. Michael Taussig, *What Color Is the Sacred?* (Chicago: University of Chicago Press, 2009), 15–16.

CHAPTER TEN

1. Berger, "Distance and Drawings," 106, 108.
2. Ibid., 116.
3. Friedrich Nietzsche, *The Birth of Tragedy and the Case of Wagner* (New York: Vintage, 1907), 50.
4. Michael Taussig, *Shamanism, Colonialism, and the Wild Man: A Study in Terror and Healing* (Chicago: University of Chicago Press, 1991), 141.
5. Ibid., 161.
6. Ibid., 154–55.
7. Ibid., 150

1. Taussig, *Shamanism*, 121, 372–74.
2. Walter Benjamin, *The Arcades Project* (Cambridge, MA: Belknap Press, 2002), 391.

1. Walter Benjamin, *On Hashish* (Cambridge, MA: Belknap Press, 2006), 81.
2. Benjamin, *On Hashish*, 71.
3. Walter Benjamin, "1932–1934 Version," in *Berlin Childhood around 1900*, trans. Howard Eiland (Cambridge, MA: Harvard University Press, 2006), 131.
4. Benjamin, *On Hashish*, 69.
5. Benjamin, "Theses on the Philosophy of History," in *Illuminations*, ed. Hannah Arendt (New York: Schocken, 1968), 263. Only "dialectical images are genuine images . . . the place where one encounters them is in language" (Benjamin, *Arcades Project*, 192).
6. Benjamin, "Surrealism," 192.
7. Benjamin, *On Hashish*, 66.
8. Benjamin, "1932–1934 Version," in *Berlin Childhood around 1900*, 131.
9. Benjamin, *On Hashish*, 19.
10. Barthes, "Deliberation," in *A Barthes Reader*, 491.

CHAPTER THIRTEEN

1. Hannah Arendt, introduction to Benjamin, *Illuminations*, 45.
2. Ibid., 46.
3. Walter Benjamin, *Walter Benjamin's Archive: Images, Texts, Signs* (New York: Verso, 2007), 151.
4. Benjamin, "Unpacking My Library," in *Illuminations*.

5. Burroughs, *Cities of the Red Night*, 43–44.
6. Ibid., 140.
7. Benjamin, "Unpacking My Library," 67.
8. Michael Taussig, *The Devil and Commodity Fetishism in South America* (Chapel Hill: University of North Carolina Press, 1980).
9. Peter Gescihere, *The Modernity of Witchcraft: Politics and the Occult in Postcolonial Africa* (Charlottesville: University of Virginia Press, 1997).
10. Benjamin, *Walter Benjamin's Archive*, 151.
11. Ibid., 152.
12. Ibid,.
13. Ibid., figure 6.1, 155.
14. *Le Corbusier Sketchbooks.* 4 vols. (Cambridge, MA: MIT Press), 1981.

CHAPTER FOURTEEN

1. Benjamin, *Walter Benjamin's Archive*, 153
2. Howard Caygill, Alex Coles, and Andrzej Klimowski, *Water Benjamin for Beginners* (Cambridge: Icon Books, 1998), 77.
3. William Burroughs, interviewed by Conrad Knickerbocker, "White Junk," in *Burroughs Live: The Collected Interviews of William S. Burroughs, 1960–1997* (New York: Semiotext(e), 2001), 69.
4. Ibid., 153
5. E. R. Leach, "Appendix 7: A Note on the Qualifications of the Author," in *Political System of Highland Burma* (Boston: Beacon Press, 1964 [1954]), 311–12.
6. Ibid., 152.
7. Simryn Gill, Australian-Malaysian artist. See my essay "Pearls," in Sydney's Museum of Contemporary Art's *Simryn Gill* (Germany: Verlag der Buchhandlung Walter Konig, n.d.), 101–13; the image here is on 21.

CHAPTER FIFTEEN

1. Roland Barthes, *Mourning Diary: October 26, 1977–September 15, 1979* (New York: Hill and Wang, 2009).
2. Barthes, "Deliberation," 491.
3. Didion, "On Keeping a Notebook," 131.
4. W. B. Yeats, *Autobiographies: The Collected Works of W. B. Yeats* (New York: Scribner, 1999), 341.
5. Didion, "On Keeping a Notebook," 131.
6. Ibid., 137.
7. Barthes, "The Third Meaning," 318.
8. Didion, "On Keeping a Notebook," 140
9. Joan Didion, *Salvador* (New York: Simon and Schuster, 1983).
10. Joan Didion, *The Year of Magical Thinking* (New York: Vintage, 2007).

11. W. G. Sebald, "Between History and Natural History: On the Literary Description of Total Destruction," in *On the Natural History of Destruction*, trans. Anthea Bell (New York: Modern Library, 2004), 60.

CHAPTER SIXTEEN

1. Walter Benjamin, "The Work of Art in the Age of Mechanical Reproduction," in *Illuminations*.
2. Ibid., 238.
3. Didion, "On Keeping a Notebook," 140.
4. Ibid., 138.
5. Muriel Gardiner, ed., *The Wolf Man by the Wolf Man* (New York: Basic Books, 1971), 145.
6. Sigmund Freud, "Studies on Hysteria," in *The Standard Edition of the Complete Psychological Works of Sigmund Freud*, ed. James Stratchey (London: Hogarth Press, 1955), 2:21–47.
7. Benjamin, "Theses on the Philosophy of History," in *Illuminations*, 255.
8. Benjamin, "Thesis XVII," 263.
9. Sigmund Freud, *Beyond the Pleasure Principle* (New York: Barnes and Noble Publishing, 2006), 18:6, 33.

CHAPTER SEVENTEEN

1. Theodor W. Adorno, *Prisms* (Cambridge, MA: MIT Press, 1981).
2. Breton, *Mad Love*, 10.
3. W. H. Auden, "Musée des Beaux Arts," in *W. H. Auden: Collected Poems*, ed. Edwards Mendelson (New York: Random House, 1976), 146–47.

CHAPTER EIGHTEEN

1. Primo Levi, interview with Philip Roth at end of *Survival in Auschwitz* (New York: Touchstone, 1995); and interview with Germaine Greer (1985), in *The Voice of Memory: Primo Levi: Interviews 1961–1987* (New York: New Press, 2001 [1997]), 3.
2. Rachel Spencer, "An Act of Bearing Witness: Primo Levi's *Survival at Auschwitz*" (class essay in "The Anthropology of Estrangement," Columbia University, September 2010).
3. Primo Levi, *The Reawakening*, trans. Stuart Woolf (New York: Simon and Schuster, 1995 [1963]), 16.
4. Ibid.
5. Levi, "Primo Levi in Conversation (Ian Thompson)," in *The Voice of Memory*, 41.

6. Primo Levi, interview with Philip Roth, "A Conversation with Primo Levi," in *Survival in Auschwitz* (London: Classic House Books, 2008), 181.

AFTERTHOUGHTS

1. Barry Miles, "The Inventive Mind of Brion Gysin," in *Brion Gysin: Tuning In to the Multimedia Age*, ed. Jose Ferez Kuri (New York: Thames and Hudson, 2003), 124.
2. See Jean-Guy Goulet and Bruce Granville Miller, *Extraordinary Anthropology: Transformations in the Field* (Lincoln: University of Nebraska Press, 2007).
3. Ibid., 137.
4. Benjamin, *Storyteller*, 89–90.

BIBLIOGRAPHY

Adorno, Theodor W. "A Portrait of Walter Benjamin." In *Prisms*. Cambridge, MA: MIT Press, 1981.

Arendt, Hannah. Introduction to *Illuminations: Essays and Reflections*, 45–46. New York: Schocken, 1969.

Artaud, Antonin. "Concerning a Journey to the Land of the Tarahumaras: The Mountain of Signs." In *Antonin Artaud Anthology*, 69. 2nd ed. San Francisco: City Light Books, 1965.

Attridge, Derek. "Roland Barthes's Obtuse, Sharp Meaning and the Responsibilities of Commentary." In *Writing the Image after Roland Barthes*, 79. Edited by Jean-Michael Rabaté. Philadelphia: University of Pennsylvania Press, 1997.

Barthes, Roland. "Deliberation." In *A Barthes Reader*, 494–95. New York: Hill and Wang, 1983.

———. *Mourning Diary: October 26, 1977–September 15, 1979*. New York: Hill and Wang, 2009.

———. *The Rustle of Language*. Oxford : Oxford University Press, 1986.

———. "The Third Meaning: Research Notes on Some Eisenstein Stills." In *A Barthes Reader*, 318. Edited by Susan Sontag. New York: Hill and Wang, 1983.

Bataille, Georges. *The Accursed Share: An Essay on General Economy Consumption*. 1976. Reprint, New York: Zone Books, 1991.

———. *Prehistoric Paintings, Lascaux, or the Birth of Art*. Geneva: Skira, 1955.

Benjamin, Walter. *The Arcades Project*. Cambridge, MA: Belknap Press, 2002.

———. *Berlin Childhood around 1900.* Translated by Howard Eiland. Cambridge, MA: Harvard University Press, 2006.

———. *Illuminations: Essays and Reflections.* New York: Schocken, 1969.

———. "1932–1934 Version." In *Berlin Childhood around 1900,* 131. Cambridge, MA: Belknap Press, 2006.

———. *On Hashish.* Cambridge, MA: Belknap Press, 2006.

———. *Reflections: Essays, Aphorisms, Autobiographical Writings.* New York: Schocken, 1986.

———. "Surrealism: Last Snapshot of the European Intelligentsia." In *Reflections.* Toronto: Harcourt Brace Jovanovich, 1978.

———. *Walter Benjamin's Archive: Images, Texts, Signs.* Edited by Ursula Marx, Gudrun Schwarz, Michael Schwarz, and Erdmut Wizisla. New York: Verso, 2007.

Berger, John. "John Berger, Life Drawing." In *Berger on Drawing,* 3. Edited by Jim Savage. Aghabullogue, Co. Cork, Ireland: Occasional Press. N.d.

———. *A Seventh Man.* New York: Viking Adult, 1975.

———. *Ways of Seeing.* Boston: Penguin, 1990.

Boas, Franz. *Franz Boas among the Inuit of Baffin Island, 1883–1884: Journals and Letters.* Toronto: University of Toronto Press, 1998.

Bohannan, Laura [Eleanor Smith Bowen, pseud.]. *Return to Laughter: An Anthropological Novel.* New York: Doubleday and the American Museum of Natural History, 1954.

Brecht, Bertolt. "Alienation Effects in the Narrative Pictures of the Elder Breughel." In *Brecht on Theater,* 157–59. 1964. Reprint, New York: Hill and Wang, 1992.

Breton, Andre. *Mad Love.* Translated by Mary Ann Caws. Lincoln: University of Nebraska Press, 1987 [1937].

Brett, Guy. "Gysin Known and Unknown: The Calligraphic Paintings." In *Brion Gysin: Tuning in to the Multimedia Age,* 56. New York: Thames & Hudson, 2003.

Burroughs, William S. *Burroughs Live: The Collected Interviews of William S. Burroughs, 1960–1997.* Brooklyn: Semiotexte, 2001.

———. *Cities of the Red Night.* Austin: Holt Rinehart & Winston, 1981.

———. Introduction to *The Last Museum,* 8. United States: Grove Press, 1986.

————. *Naked Lunch: The Restored Text*. New York: Grove Press, 2001.

————. "Ports of Entry: Here Is Space-Time Painting." In *Brion Gysin: Tuning in to the Multimedia Age*, 29–38. New York: Thames & Hudson, 2003.

————. *Queer: A Novel*. Boston: Penguin, 1987.

————. *The Western Lands*. New York: Viking Penguin, 1987.

————. "William S. Burroughs, The Art of Fiction No. 36." Interview by Conrad Knickerbocker. *Paris Review* 35 (Fall 1965).

Burroughs, William S., and Brion Gysin. *The Third Mind*. New York: Viking, 1978.

Burroughs, William S., and Robert A. Sobieszek. *Ports of Entry: William S. Burroughs and the Arts*. Jerusalem: Small Press Distribution, 1996.

Caygill, Howard, Alex Coles, and Andrzej Klimowski. *Water Benjamin for Beginners*. Cambridge: Icon Books, 1998.

Crapanzano, Vincent. "At the Heart of the Discipline." In *Emotions in the Field: The Psychology and Anthropology of Fieldwork Experience*, 60–61. Stanford: Stanford University Press, 2010.

Derrida, Jacques. *Memoirs of the Blind: The Self-Portrait and Other Ruins*. Chicago: University of Chicago Press, 1993.

Didion, Joan. "On Keeping a Notebook." In *Slouching Towards Bethlehem: Essays*, 131–41. New York: Farrar, Straus and Giroux, 1968.

————. *Salvador*. New York: Simon and Schuster, 1983.

————. *The Year of Magical Thinking*. New York: Vintage, 2007.

Dubovsky, Anthony. "The Euphoria of the Everyday." In *Drawing/Thinking: Confronting an Electronic Age*, ed. 72–81. New York: Routledge, 2008.

Evans-Pritchard, E. E. *Witchcraft, Oracles, and Magic among the Azande*. Oxford: Clarendon Press, 1951.

Forero, Juan. "As Colombian War Crimes Suspects Sit in U.S. Jails, Victims' Kin Protest." Washingtonpost.com. http://www.washingtonpost.com/wp-dyn/content/article/2009/10/03/AR2009100303001.html (accessed October 5, 2009).

Freud, Sigmund. *Beyond the Pleasure Principle*. New York: Barnes & Noble Publishing, 2006.

————. "Studies on Hysteria." Vol. 2 of *The Standard Edition of the Complete Psychological Works of Sigmund Freud*, 21–47. Edited by James

Stratchey. Richmond: Hogarth Press and the Institute of Psycho-Analysis, 1968.

———. *The Wolf Man by the Wolf Man with the Case of the Wolf Man*. New York: Basic Books, 1971.

Gandolfo, Daniella. *The City at Its Limits: Taboo, Transgression, and Urban Renewal in Lima*. Chicago: University of Chicago Press, 2009.

Geiger, John Grisby. "Brion Gysin: His Life and Times." In *Brion Gysin: Tuning in to the Multimedia Age*, 204–16. New York: Thames & Hudson, 2003.

Genet, Jean. *Prisoner of Love*. New York: New York Review Books, 2003.

Geschiere, Peter. *The Modernity of Witchcraft: Politics and the Occult in Postcolonial Africa (Sorcellerie Et Politique En Afrique-La Viande Des Autres)*. Charlottesville: University of Virginia Press, 1997.

Gill, Simryn. *Pearls*. New York: Raking Leaves, 2008.

Goulet, Jean-Guy, and Bruce Granville Miller. *Extraordinary Anthropology: Transformations in the Field*. Lincoln: University of Nebraska Press, 2007.

Grubbs, Christopher. "Drawing Life, Drawing Ideas." In *Drawing/Thinking: Confronting an Electronic Age*, 105. New York: Routledge, 2008.

Gumpert, Lynn. "From Concept to Object: The Artistic Practice of Drawing." In *Drawing/Thinking: Confronting an Electronic Age*, 46–59. New York: Routledge, 2008.

Gunn, Wendy, ed. *Fieldnotes and Sketchbooks*. Frankfurt: Peter Lang, 2009.

Gysin, Brion. *The Process*. New York: Doubleday, 1969.

———. *To Master — A Long Goodnight: The Story of Uncle Tom, A Historical Narrative*. New York: Creative Age Press, 1949.

Gysin, Brion, and Terry Wilson. *Here to Go: Planet R-101, Brion Gysin interviewed by Terry Wilson*. San Francisco: RE/Search Publications, 1982.

Harris, Oliver. *The Letters of William S. Burroughs 1945–1959*. New York: Viking Press, 1993.

Hoffman, Laura. "Disappearing Act: The Art of Brion Gysin." In *Brion Gysin: Dream Machine*, 57–143. New York: New Museum, 2010.

Hoffmann, Roald. *The Same and Not the Same*. New York: Columbia University Press, 1997.

Holcomb, Melanie. *Pen and Parchment: Drawing in the Middle Ages.* New York: Metropolitan Museum of Art, 2009.

Jackson, Jean. "I Am a Fieldnote: Fieldnotes as a Symbol of Professional Identity." In *Fieldnotes: The Makings of Anthropology*, 28–30. Ithaca: Cornell University Press, 1990.

Le Corbusier Sketchbooks. Vol. 1, *1914–1948.* Edited by Fondation Le Corbusier. London: MIT Press, 1981.

Leach, E. R. *Political Systems of Highland Burma: A Study of Kachin Social Structure.* Boston: Beacon Press, 1967.

Levi, Primo. *The Reawakening.* New York: Touchstone, 1995.

———. *Survival in Auschwitz.* London: Classic House Books, 2008.

———. *The Voice of Memory: Interviews, 1961–1987.* New York: New Press, 2002.

McDermott, Jeremy. "Toxic Fallout of Colombian Scandal." BBC News. http://news.bbc.co.uk/2/hi/americas/8038399.stm (accessed May 8, 2009).

Miles, Barry. *A Descriptive Catalogue of the William S. Burroughs Archive.* New York: Covent Garden Press, 1974.

———. "The Inventive Mind of Brion Gysin." In *Brion Gysin: Tuning in to the Multimedia Age*, 124. New York: Thames and Hudson, 2003.

Mina, Mateo. *Esclavitud y libertad en el Valle del rio Cauca.* Bogota: Fundación Rosca, 1975.

Nietzsche, Friedrich. *The Birth of Tragedy.* New York: Vintage, 1966.

———. *On the Genealogy of Morals and Ecce Homo.* New York: Vintage Books, 1969.

———. *The Twilight of the Idols and the Anti-Christ; or, How to Philosophize with a Hammer.* Reissue ed. London: Penguin, 1990.

Olin, Laurie. "More Than Rigging Your Wrist (or Your Mouse): Thinking, Seeing, and Drawing." In *Drawing/Thinking: Confronting an Electronic Age*, 82. New York: Routledge, 2008.

Ottenberg, Simon. "Thirty Years of Fieldnotes: Changing Relationships to the Text." In *Fieldnotes: The Makings of Anthropology*, 139–60. Ithaca: Cornell University Press, 1990.

Paumgarten, Nick. "Acts of God." *New Yorker*, July 12, 2010.

Plath, David W. "Field Notes, Filed Notes, and the Conferring of Note." In *Fieldnotes: The Makings of Anthropology*, 378. Ithaca: Cornell University Press, 1990.

Rulfo, Juan. *Pedro Paramo*. 1955. Reprint ed. Madrid: Editorial Debate, 2000.

Sebald, W. G. "Between History and Natural History: On the Literary Description of Total Destruction." In *On the Natural History of Destruction*. Translated by Anthea Bell. New York: Modern Library, 2004.

Speck, Frank G. *Naskapi: The Savage Hunters of the Labrador Peninsula*. 3rd ed. Norman: University of Oklahoma Press, 1978.

Srinivas, M. N. *The Remembered Village*. Berkeley: University of California Press, 1980.

Sullivan, Chip. "Telling Untold Stories." In *Drawing/Thinking: Confronting an Electronic Age*, 122–35. New York: Routledge, 2008.

Taussig, Michael. *Defacement: Public Secrecy and the Labor of the Negative*. Stanford: Stanford University Press, 1999.

——— . *The Devil and Commodity Fetishism in South America*. Chapel Hill: University of North Carolina Press, 1980.

———. *Mimesis and Alterity: A Particular History of the Senses*. New York: Routledge, 1992.

———. *Shamanism, Colonialism, and the Wild Man: A Study in Terror and Healing*. Chicago: University of Chicago Press, 1991.

———. *Walter Benjamin's Grave*. Chicago: University of Chicago Press, 2006.

———. *What Color Is the Sacred?* Chicago: University of Chicago Press, 2009.

Wilkinson, Daniel. "Death and Drugs in Colombia." *New York Review of Books*, August 18, 2011.

Yeats, William Butler. *Autobiographies: The Collected Works of W. B. Yeats*. Vol. 3. New York: Scribner, 1999.

Lightning Source UK Ltd.
Milton Keynes UK
UKOW02f1329130116

266324UK00001B/101/P